INPUT-OUTPUT ANALYSIS AND
RESOURCE ALLOCATION

INPUT-OUTPUT ANALYSIS
AND RESOURCE
ALLOCATION

BURGESS CAMERON

Department of Economics
Australian National University

CAMBRIDGE
AT THE UNIVERSITY PRESS
1968

Published by the Syndics of the Cambridge University Press
Bentley House, 200 Euston Road, London, N.W.1
American Branch: 32 East 57th Street, New York, N.Y.10022

Library of Congress Catalogue Card Number: 68–21188
Standard Book Number: 521 071143

Printed in Great Britain
at the University Printing House, Cambridge
(Brooke Crutchley, University Printer)

CONTENTS

Preface   *page* vii

Introduction   1

1   The Theory of Employment   4

2   Input-Output Analysis   10

3   Application   19

4   Technology   40

5   Maximum Production with Two Scarce Resources   46

6   Tastes   62

7   Development   68

8   International Trade   81

9   Conclusion   93

Appendix: Determinants and Matrices   96

List of Symbols   105

Bibliography   107

Index   109

PREFACE

The reader is assumed to be familar with the Keynesian theory that an adequate level of aggregate final demand is necessary for the full employment of the work force. In other words, *adequate demand is one condition for national economic efficiency*. Using the Keynesian system as a starting point, this book develops the concept of an economic system in order to analyse other conditions for national economic efficiency. It is assumed that production processes yield constant scale returns and that consumer goods are demanded in specified proportions (but not in chapter 6). These assumptions enable us to retain much of the inherent simplicity of Keynesian economics while analysing the basic issues of efficient resource allocation.

This book is a logical successor to my earlier work, *The Determination of Production*, now out of print. Chapters 6 and 8 of the present study are drawn to some extent from the earlier book.

Chapter 3 explores some applications of input-output analysis and can be omitted by the reader who does not wish to explore the practical problems discussed.

I am indebted to the editors of the *Economic Record* and of the *International Economic Review* for permission to use material which first appeared in those journals. I am also indebted to Jill Pertoldi for her devoted editorial assistance. My greatest debt, however, is to the modern practitioners of empirical general equilibrium analysis, for without their energy and insight we might still be contemplating Walras' *Eléments*.

BURGESS CAMERON

INTRODUCTION

Perhaps the most respectable reason for studying economics stems from a desire to ensure that economies operate as efficiently as possible. The conditions for national efficiency are many: adequate final demand for commodities; avoidance of production bottlenecks; adequate incentives to ensure that business managers both respond to demand and organize their plant efficiently; the availability of effective methods of choice between alternative methods of production; the opportunity for consumers to choose between commodities so as to maximize their satisfaction; rational choice in framing the nation's long-term investment programme; the need to choose an optimal size and composition of foreign trade (so that the economy may trade as far as possible out beyond its production possibility curve); the avoidance of monopolistic restrictions in resource supply, in access to methods of production and in production of commodities; the avoidance of excessive surplus capacity. This list is doubtless incomplete and of course efficiency is not the sole criterion by which to judge the performance of an economy—inequality of opportunity or of wealth are others.

In order to approach the subject of national economic efficiency, Keynes' one-industry one-resource model of an economy is extended to multi-sectoral analysis in chapter 2 and the application of these ideas is examined in chapter 3. Up to this stage the analysis is simplified inasmuch as a variety of choices by resource owners, businessmen and consumers are assumed predetermined. Subsequently, as the argument is made increasingly realistic by the recognition of opportunities for choice, we explore the implications of specifying the objective of maximum national product. Thus in chapter 5, the composition of the final bill of goods is given but there is opportunity for choice between alternative methods of production with different land/labour input ratios. It is obvious in principle that from a knowledge of available resources we should be able to specify the methods of production which will yield the maximum national product. It turns out that there are four lines of reasoning which enable us to specify this maximum national product. The method of analysis set out in this chapter is then applied to problems of development and trade.

TABLE 1. *Transactions Table 1953–54 Purchaser's Values, £m.*
(Australia)

	1	2	3	4	5	6	7	8	9	10	11	12	13	14	15
1. Sheep	.	.	.	1	.	.	.	84	.	.	.	.	.	.	.
2. Other rural	8	63	32	205	30	3	17	11	..	1	..	1	1	..	..
3. Beer, tobacco	.	.	9	..	.	.	.	..	.	.	.	.	.	.	.
4. Foodstuffs	9	33	4	74	.	.	1	.	.	.	.	.	.	.	.
5. Woodworking	.	..	..	3	54	1	3	..	2	2	1	.	..	2	1
6. Paper	.	.	3	16	..	64	8	3	.	.	.	.	.	1	.
7. Chemicals	9	20	5	8	1	3	77	3	1	3	..	.	.	1	13
8. Textiles	5	8	.	5	1	.	9	205	.	.	.	..	.	.	.
9. Coal	.	.	1	4	..	1	3	1	1	1	..	52	1	..	..
10. Other mining	.	.	.	.	..	.	18	.	.	76	.	.	11	12	2
11. Oil refining	10	29	..	2	1	..	3	1	.	2	17	6	1	..	..
12. Gas, electricity	.	.	1	6	2	2	6	3	1	5	..	4	14	1	2
13. Iron and steel	.	.	.	.	.	.	.	.	.	.	.	.	84	1	6
14. Radio and electrical	.	.	..	1	..	..	1	..	.	.	.	1	..	39	..
15. Motor vehicles	.	.	.	.	.	.	.	.	.	.	.	.	.	.	148
16. Other engineering	27	29	2	26	4	2	9	5	6	17	2	5	3	2	5
17. Building materials and building	.	1	.	.	.	..	.	.	.	.	..	.	1	.	.
18. Transport	15	50	5	33	9	3	16	13	28	14	20	3	5	1	10
19. Commerce	86	139	94	114	33	20	73	164	..	2	64	28	.	10	51
20. Services	7	19	4	59	26	9	56	54	5	12	5	6	3	17	15
Employment '000	179	318	14	108	80	56	84	197	28	46	2	18	20	48	90
Wages	46	76	11	75	52	42	64	115	27	42	2	16	19	36	62
Profits	273	328	10	49	21	24	36	40	13	28	7	15	8	9	18
Depreciation	20	65	1	7	2	3	7	4	2	4	1	6	2	2	3
Net indirect taxes	16	2	132	18	10	7	31	22	2	3	34	1	2	8	36
Non-competing imports	.	.	.	.	.	.	8	7	.	4	10	.	.	.	.
Competing imports	2	36	7	25	19	37	86	124	..	18	84	..	19	25	70
Total cost of supplies net	532	834	313	659	211	156	454	656	86	158	230	140	90	129	294

2

16	17	18	19	20	Private consumption	Government* consumption	Fixed investment†	Exports	Stocks	Total sales	
.	.	.	.	.	77	.	.	386	−16	532	1. Sheep
..	1	1	.	68	293	17	.	106	+41	834	2. Other rural
.	.	.	.	.	307	.	.	2	+4	313	3. Beer, tobacco
.	.	1	3	40	378	19	.	156	+17	659	4. Foodstuffs
3	111	1	3	15	52	3	.	3	+4	211	5. Woodworking
.	2	1	23	31	62	2	.	2	+2	156	6. Paper
3	37	8	6	98	187	7	.	19	+21	454	7. Chemicals
.	..	2	3	121	389	20	.	51	+41	656	8. Textiles
1	5	14	.	..	.	..	.	2	+..	86	9. Coal
29	30	1	.	1	.	..	.	65	−11	158	10. Other mining
4	2	31	9	57	52	4	.	1	+14	230	11. Oil refining
7	2	8	14	6	59	2	.	..	−1	140	12. Gas, electricity
67	7	..	.	.	.	.	.	11	−2	90	13. Iron and steel
10	6	..	..	14	59	1	31	1	+2	129	14. Radio and electrical
.	.	11	4	..	60	..	216	2	+1	294	15. Motor vehicles
78	44	15	1	36	133	5	269	17	+5	671	16. Other engineering
.	92	..	.	5	43	1	621	1	−37	636	17. Building materials and building
21	5	.	.	58	107	.	.	.	.	417	18. Transport
85	12	.	.	.	.	.	.	.	.	974	19. Commerce
48	27	11	109	*130*	462	31	.	73	.	1056	20. Services
224	341	287	600	443	35	395	.	.	.	3612	Empoyment '000
171	219	240	362	223	16	316	.	.	.	2233	Wages
41	106	48	396	165	.	.	.	.	.	1634	Profits
6	2	13	18	33	.	.	.	.	.	200	Depreciation
28	7	11	22	29	37	.	.	.	.	458	Net indirect taxes
.	.	.	.	.	.	.	.	.	.	30	Non-competing imports
146	9	.	.	56	.	.	.	.	.	763	Competing imports
671	636	417	974	1056	2772	428	1137	898	83		Total cost of supplies net

* Current Government expenditure on goods and services.
† Gross Private Investment in fixed capital equipment *plus* public works.

A single dot in the table indicates a zero entry, a double dot indicates less than £0·5 million. Due to rounding, columns and rows may not add to totals.

The italicized entries in the principal diagonal are internal sales. The column and row sums are net of these internal sales.

The row for employment includes both employers and employees. Wages, however, are the income of employees only.

3

1

THE THEORY OF EMPLOYMENT

1. Introduction

The attempt to ensure that a nation is producing the greatest possible level of production (within the limits set by social institutions and the desire for leisure) involves two separable problems. The first is to ensure that all available resources are employed in industry. The second is to ensure that those resources are employed as productively as possible.

The theory of employment of J. M. Keynes is concerned with the first of these problems. For simplicity, Keynes regarded the entire industrial structure as a single giant industry and assumed that labour was the sole variable scarce resource used by this industry. He then successfully argued that some of the work force may remain unemployed because the level of demand for commodities is not high enough to buy all supplies at full employment production.[1]

We will not recapitulate Keynes' entire theory here. However, it is useful to list the basic elements of his analysis: specified variable resources (labour) are available for employment in industry; in the existing state of technology there is a certain volume of national production producible by any stated volume of employed labour; the national income comprises the national wage-bill and the gross operating surplus (or profit) which we may assume for simplicity to be determined by a fixed percentage profit markup on wages; and finally the level of final demand for commodities, particularly the level of consumer demand, depends on various influences of which the most important is the level of personal disposable income. These four elements are drawn upon in order to specify the equilibrium level of employment and output, defined as the level at which aggregate demand equals aggregate supply. Since this equilibrium level of output may not coincide with full employment, Keynes and his followers were then concerned with the ways in which full employment might be achieved by raising demand.

[1] See J. M. Keynes, *The General Theory of Employment, Interest and Money*, Macmillan, London, 1936.

The four data just listed—resource availability, the state of technology, the degree of competition (as indicated by the size of the profit markup), and the nature of tastes determining final demand—are the basic elements of any analysis of the operation of an entire economy.

In practice it is convenient to record these four data in functional form. The availability of a resource may be recorded in a factor supply function showing the amount of the factor supplied at each price of factor services; in the case of labour we will here assume for simplicity that the whole of the work force ω is available for employment at any wage-rate it can obtain. The state of technology may be recorded in a production function showing the maximum amount producible[1] from any given combination of productive factors; here we may assume that the production function relating employment (N) to national product (X), $N = a_{ni}X$, is characterized by a constant labour input coefficient a_{ni}.[2] The degree of competition may be recorded in the form of an entry function (showing the ease with which new firms may enter the industry) which in its simplest form specifies a normal or established percentage profit mark-up on costs; here the profit mark-up (s) on the wage bill determines the price level[3] as seen from the cost account: (P being the price level and P_n the wage-rate)

$$XP \equiv (N.P_n)(1+s).$$

Fourthly, the state of consumer tastes is recorded by the consumption function which here shows the volume of consumption at constant prices (C) to be determined by real income—the term in square brackets being national income

$$\frac{(C.P)}{P} = a + c\frac{[(N.P_n)(1+s)]}{P}.$$

Investment demand in real terms (I) is here treated as a parameter.

Having assembled these four sets of data we can explore the characteristics of market equilibrium by feeding the data into the condition of market equilibrium that planned demand equals supply, i.e.

$$C+I = X.$$

---

[1] 'Maximum' here implies avoidance of waste, not an optimal choice between efficient activities.   [2] For meaning of symbols, see p. 105.
[3] It also determines the distribution of income between wages and profits.

Before doing so, however, it should be noted that in such a model of the economy, one final demand function or one factor supply function is always superfluous since the level of production is limited either by final demand or by factor supply, but not by both. Since Keynes wrote his theory to explain mass unemployment, the labour supply function was implicitly regarded as redundant. However, our later analysis will cover cases of both unemployment and full employment.[1]

In the Keynesian system just outlined, the consumption function may be re-written, using the cost account, in the form

$$C = a + cX.$$

Substituting this in the condition of market equilibrium we obtain the solution value for equilibrium national product

$$X = (a+I) . \frac{1}{1-c}. \tag{1}$$

From the production function we thus obtain the equilibrium level of employment

$$N = a_{ni}(a+I) . \frac{1}{1-c},$$

which here we assume will be found to be less than the work force ω.

2. Properties of the single industry model[2]

Diverging briefly from the main argument, it is worthwhile illustrating the versatility of Keynes' construction and the insight into practical economic problems that it gives with relatively simple modifications.

First, if we call X_{FE} the full employment output producible by the work force ω, then the level of planned investment consistent with full employment is $[(1-c) . X_{FE}] - a.$

Second, there is the famous multiplier analysis stemming from the first difference of equation (1)

$$\Delta X = \Delta I . \frac{1}{1-c} \tag{2}$$

---

[1] Theories of inflation which use the concept of forced savings implicitly treat a consumption function as redundant, while the factor supply function specifies maximum attainable output.
[2] This section may be omitted on a first reading.

indicating, since $0 < c < 1$, that a fall in real investment will have a multiplied effect on production.

Third, we may introduce government spending on goods and services (G) as a parameter, as well as an income tax rate (t) so we have the concept of after-tax income or personal disposable income (PDI)

$$PDI = (1-t)(X.P).$$

It is then more realistic to re-state the consumption function to show consumption spending as a function of personal disposable income

$$\frac{(C.P)}{P} = a+c\frac{(PDI)}{P}.$$

Hence $\qquad\qquad C = a+c(1-t)X.$

In addition foreign trade can be introduced, for the present, regarding the quantity of exports (E) as a parameter and the quantity of imports (M) as a fixed proportion (m) of home production,

$$M = mX.$$

Then by substituting this information into the condition of market equilibrium

$$C+I+G+E = X+M,$$

and assuming that all final demand has the same import content, we obtain the solution value for equilibrium national product

$$X = \frac{a+I+G+E}{(1+m)}\cdot\frac{1}{1-c'},$$

where c' is the marginal propensity to consume home-produced goods out of national income (or, the ratio of the increment in consumption demand for home-produced goods to the small unit increment in national income causing that rise in demand). A first difference of this is

$$\Delta X = \frac{\Delta I}{(1+m)}\cdot\frac{1}{1-c'} \qquad (3)$$

a result, essentially similar to equation (2), indicating that when a sustained autonomous fall in investment demand occurs in an under-employed economy, that part of the investment which is a fall in demand for the produce of home labour will have a multiplier effect on national product, whose value is given by $1/(1-c')$.

The conclusion in equation (3) is still at an elementary level of analysis since it ignores: the foreign trade multiplier,[1] the co-existence of foreign trade disequilibrium with market equilibrium,[2] and feed-back effects due to the liquidity preference function.[3] Modifications to recognise these are important for economic policy.

Another modification of the original model is to recognize that recipients of wages (W) and profits (S) have different marginal propensities to consume, so that the consumption function is re-written

$$\frac{(C.P)}{P} = a+b.\frac{S}{P}+c.\frac{W}{P}.$$

By substituting this into the condition of market equilibrium

$$C+I = X,$$

we obtain the solution value

$$X = (a+I)\left[\frac{1}{1-c+(c-b)p}\right],$$

where the profit share p of national income is defined

$$p \equiv \frac{s}{1+s} \quad (s \text{ being the profit mark-up on wages}).$$

This provides a basis for estimating the deflationary effect of a shift to profits if $c > b$.

Finally, the basic Keynesian model may be modified by the introduction of further demand functions. For example, the introduction of investment demand as a function of the growth of national product introduces the concept of a shifting equilibrium and the specification of the equilibrium growth rate of national product.[4]

---

[1] See F. Machlup, *International Trade and the National Income Multiplier*, A. M. Kelley, New York, 1961.

[2] See T. W. Swan, 'Longer-Run Problems of the Balance of Payments', chapter 24 in *The Australian Economy*, ed. H. W. Arndt and W. M. Corden, F. W. Cheshire, Melbourne, 1963.

[3] See J. M. Keynes, *The General Theory of Employment, Interest and Money*, Macmillan, London, 1936.

[4] See E. Domar, *Essays in the Theory of Economic Growth*, Oxford Univ. Press, New York, 1957, chapter 4.

3. Conclusion

Keynes' assumption of a single giant industry is a tremendous abstraction which conceals, or rather postpones, important problems. For example, if we wish to raise employment by raising demand for output, we need to recognize that the labour used per unit of output varies in different industries. Moreover, if we are already near full employment, the level of output in one industry may be restricted not by demand but by non-delivery of raw materials from another industry due to scarcity of labour or plant capacity. In short, once the basic insights of Keynes' single industry economy have been gained, there are strong grounds for wanting to develop the argument to a many-industry economy.

This extension to a many-industry model of the economy can readily be achieved. For example, if the economy consisted of thirty industries then the following relations should be set out:[1] for each industry both the state of technology and the competitive organisation of the industry should be specified as well as the influences determining the demand for its output; to these three pieces of information we add the equilibrium condition that demand for and supply of each commodity are equal; finally, the availability of each scarce resource must be specified.

It may seem surprising that by a mere process of duplicating sets of relations for each industry, we can describe an economy where the available resources are employed by the complex of industries which turn out the final product. In fact, however, these relations or equations form an interdependent system both because the industries use common resources, because they purchase materials from one another and because their products compete for the consumer's dollar. The solution of this system for equilibrium levels of output will be illustrated in the next chapter.

[1] It is implicitly assumed here that each industry produces one commodity and each commodity is produced by one industry. However, the analysis can be extended to cover joint production.

2

INPUT-OUTPUT ANALYSIS

1. Levels of Output

We begin by setting out the system of relations for a hypothetical economy having three industries. Each industry has a specified method of production characterised by constant scale returns (i.e. doubling all variable inputs doubles the output) and fixed factor proportions—hence the technical input coefficients (the amount of input of a factor per unit of output) are fixed. For simplicity, the quantity of a commodity demanded by consumers is assumed to depend only on their real income, and real investment demand is assumed to be known. There is no joint production, each industry producing its 'own' commodity. The only scarce resource is homogenous labour and it is assumed that the entire work force is available for employment for any wage it can obtain.

Numbering the industries 1, 2, 3, the system of equations for the first industry comprises the state of technology described by a list of input coefficients a_{ij}; the demand function for its product; and the condition that the sum of all demands equals output in equilibrium. These relations are:

Industry 1

$$\left.\begin{array}{l} a_{11}X_1 = x_{11};\ a_{21}X_1 = x_{21};\ a_{31}X_1 = x_{31};\ a_{n1}X_1 = x_{n1}; \\ C_1 = b_1 + c_1Y'; \\ X_1 = x_{11} + x_{12} + x_{13} + C_1 + I_1; \end{array}\right\} \quad (1)$$

a_{ij} is the input of i per unit of output of j,

x_{ij} is the input of i used in producing j,

X_j is the output of commodity j,

C_i, I_i are the quantities of consumption and investment demand for i,

Y' is national income Y divided by a price index,

b, c are constants.

A similar set of relations is written down for each of the other industries.

The entire array of relations may be re-written more compactly by writing down the set of equilibrium conditions, i.e. one for each industry, and then substituting all the other data on technology and demand into these equilibrium equations. The result, assuming $a_{ii} = 0$, may be written[1]

$$
\left.\begin{aligned}
b_1 + c_1 Y' + I_1 &= X_1 - a_{12} X_2 - a_{13} X_3 \\
b_2 + c_2 Y' + I_2 &= -a_{21} X_1 + X_2 - a_{23} X_3 \\
b_3 + c_3 Y' + I_3 &= -a_{31} X_1 - a_{32} X_2 + X_3
\end{aligned}\right\} \tag{2}
$$

to which we add the remaining relation

$$
k = a_{n1} X_1 + a_{n2} X_2 + a_{n3} X_3 \text{ at full employment,} \tag{3}
$$

where k is the known work force.

Since the real national income Y' is a weighted linear sum of the levels of output of all industries,[2] it follows that the set of equations (2) is a set of three equations in the three unknown levels of output X_i. Assuming these linear equations to be consistent and independent, a unique solution may be obtained.

It is of course by no means necessary, or even likely, that these solution values for the levels of output will be found to produce full

---

[1] Note in this set that if there were only one industry, the second and third equations disappear, and in the first equation the coefficients a_{ij} are all zero. Since X_1 equals Y' in this case, we have the basic Keynesian system with solution
$$
Y' = \frac{b_1 + I_1}{1 - c_1}.
$$

[2] Assuming profits in industry i to be fixed as a percentage mark-up s_i on other costs, the national income
$$
Y = \sum_i (x_{ni} P_n + s_1(x_{ni} . P_n + \sum_j x_{ji} . P_j))
$$
$$
= \sum_i a_{ni} . X_i (1 + s_i + s_i \sum_j (a_{ji}/a_{ni}) . P_j)
$$
the wage rate ($P_n = 1$) being used as numéraire. In this expression sigma i gives the summation for all industries, sigma j gives the summation for all cost items j (materials, fuel) used in the industry. It will be shown later that equilibrium commodity prices are determinate and may therefore be treated here as known.

Real national income $\qquad Y' = Y/P,$

where the price index $\qquad P = \sum_i w_i . P_i,$

w_i being appropriate weights.

11

employment when fed into equation (3). If the demand for labour implicit in the solution values for industrial output is much less than the work force, there is likely to be a government move to raise the level of demand. If the implied demand for labour exceeds the work force then some final demands for commodities must be reduced to a level which is feasible in terms of available resources.

2. The income multiplier

Since the many-industry model here discussed includes a set of consumption demand functions, it follows that the Keynesian multiplier is operating in comparable fashion to a single industry model. We shall illustrate this with an arithmetic example for an imaginary four-industry economy for which the data are as follows:

Technology

The four industries are wheat growing, flour-milling, black coal mining and electricity generation from coal.[1]

The wheat industry uses 100 men per unit of output.

The flour industry uses 50 units of wheat, 20 units of coal, 60 units of electricity and 200 men per unit of output.

The coal industry uses 10 men per unit of output.

The electricity industry uses 0·5 units of coal and 2 men per unit of output.

Profit

Each industry has a 20 % profit mark-up on costs.

Demand

The consumption expenditure functions in this case are (there being no consumption demand for whole wheat),

$$\text{Flour:} \qquad C_f P_f = 0·6Y,$$
$$\text{Coal:} \qquad C_c P_c = 0·1Y,$$
$$\text{Electricity:} \quad C_e P_e = 0·2Y.$$

The quantity of each commodity consumed (C_i) is thus responsive to the national income (Y) and to its own price (P_i), while aggregate consumption spending is 90 % of income. It is assumed that the only

---

[1] Their output is measured in: wheat, million bushels; flour, million short tons; coal, thousand tons; electricity, in million kwh. All outputs and inputs are measured on an annual basis.

investment demand is to stockpile coal and that this is initially 200 units per year, subsequently falling to 195 units per year.

The work force is 20,000 men, all of whom are available at the prevailing wage-rate.

From the above information we can calculate the equilibrium commodity prices in wage-units by a method set out in section 4 below as: wheat, 120 wage-units; flour, 8,419 wage-units; coal, 12 wage-units; electricity, 9·6 wage-units. (These are the prices per physical unit, e.g. the price of flour is 8,419 wage-units per million short tons.)

Also we can set out the expression for national income (Y) as a weighted sum of levels of industrial output:[1]

$$Y = 120X_w + 1{,}603{\cdot}2X_f + 12X_c + 3{\cdot}6X_e.$$

It will be seen that we can now substitute both the equilibrium prices and this expression for Y in the consumption functions so that the quantity of consumption (C_i) for each commodity is expressed as a function of levels of industrial output. If this revised form of the consumption functions, together with the data on technology, are substituted into the equilibrium condition

$$X_i = C_i + I_i + \sum_j a_{ij}.X_j$$

for each industry, we obtain the set of equations, similar to equation (2) above,

$$
\left.
\begin{aligned}
0 &= X_w - 50X_f, \\
\frac{0{\cdot}6}{8{,}419}(120X_w + 1{,}603{\cdot}2X_f + 12X_c + 3{\cdot}6X_e) & \\
&= X_f, \\
\frac{0{\cdot}1}{12}(120X_w + 1{,}603{\cdot}2X_f + 12X_c + 3{\cdot}6X_e) + I_c & \\
&= -20X_f + X_c - 0{\cdot}5X_e, \\
\frac{0{\cdot}2}{9{\cdot}6}(120X_w + 1{,}603{\cdot}2X_f + 12X_c + 3{\cdot}6X_e) & \\
&= -60X_f + X_e.
\end{aligned}
\right\} \quad (4)
$$

For an annual rate of stockpiling of coal $I_c = 200$, this yields the solution for the quantities of output of: wheat 85·544, flour 1·7109,

---

[1] See above, section 1, p. 11, footnote 2.

coal 735·68, and electricity 602·79 units; with a total employment of 17,459 persons. However, if the rate of stockpiling is reduced to $I_c = 195$ these equilibrium levels of output fall to: wheat 83·406, flour 1·6681, coal 717·29, and electricity 587·72 units. This general decline in output in all industries is due to the national income multiplier which in this example has a value of 10.[1]

The employment multiplier will only have the same value if all final commodities have the same labour content.[2] In the present example, the 5 unit fall in investment demand for coal involves a primary fall in employment of 50 men. However, employment throughout the economy ultimately falls by 437 men, from 17,459 to 17,022. In short, the employment multiplier is approximately 8·7. The employment multiplier is somewhat lower than the income multiplier because the investment good coal has a relatively high labour content (viz. $\frac{100}{120}$ or 83·3% because of the 20% profit mark-up) whereas the major consumption good flour has a lower labour content of 69% because the profit mark-up in the flour industry is applied to the cost of raw materials which themselves include profit mark-ups.[3]

3. The open model

The so-called 'open' input-output model is one in which all final demands are given. Thus final demand is a list or bill of goods and the open model is a special case of the more general model discussed above.

To illustrate the open model we will use the four-industry economy of the previous section. The same array of technical input coefficients is assumed with the addition that a unit of output of coal also uses an input of 0·005 units of electricity in the mines. We will also assume

---

[1] If the consumption functions were to include constant terms then the decline in the consumption goods industries would be proportionally less than the decline in the investment goods industries. The model can be adjusted to illustrate this.

[2] For estimating the employment multiplier from $1/(1-c)$, c is the sum of the weighted marginal propensities to spend on individual consumer goods. The weights are the ratio of a commodity's (direct and indirect) labour content to its price, divided by the ratio of the national wage bill to the national income. (It is assumed that labour input coefficients are constant.) See B. Cameron, 'Input Output Analysis', *Economic Record*, May 1954, p. 43.

[3] Labour content is calculated by computing the inverse and applying labour input coefficients. This is set out below, see p. 15.

that this is now a trading economy exporting wheat and flour, while it is assumed that one-third of coal supplies are imported (i.e. imports equal one-half home production). Since the basic equilibrium condition for each industry is that

$$D_i = X_i(1+m_i) - \sum_j a_{ij}.X_j,$$

where D_i is the final demand (consumption plus investment plus exports) for commodity i in physical units, and quantity of imports $M_i = m_i.X_i$, the set of equilibrium conditions for the four industries is

$$
\left.
\begin{aligned}
D_w &= X_w - 50X_f, \\
D_f &= \quad X_f, \\
D_c &= \quad -20X_f + 1{\cdot}5X_c - 0{\cdot}5X_e, \\
D_e &= \quad -60X_f - 0{\cdot}005X_c + X_e.
\end{aligned}
\right\} \tag{5}
$$

Instead of solving this set of equations for a specific final bill of goods, it may be more convenient to compute a general solution or inverse which has the form:[1]

$$
\left.
\begin{aligned}
X_w &= D_w + \quad 50D_f \\
X_f &= \quad\quad D_f \\
X_c &= \quad 33{\cdot}39D_f + 0{\cdot}667D_c + 0{\cdot}33D_e \\
X_e &= \quad 60{\cdot}17D_f + 0{\cdot}003D_c + \quad D_e.
\end{aligned}
\right\} \tag{6}
$$

The economic meaning of the figures in this set of equations is that, whereas the input co-efficients in equations (5) show the on-site demands for materials and other inputs, the matching coefficients in this general solution show *the sum of the on-site and off-site demands for home-produced inputs* required to satisfy unit final demand. For example, flourmilling uses 20 coal directly (on-site) and $0{\cdot}5 \times 60$ coal indirectly (off-site) through the use of electricity, a total of 50. But only two-thirds of coal supplies are home produced, so that the implied direct and indirect demand for home-produced coal is 33.33. The total figure is slightly higher at 33.39 because the coal industry itself uses electricity, i.e. there is a relation of interdependence between the coal and electricity industries so that any direct demand

---

[1] See Appendix, p. 103, for calculation.

for coal implies an indirect demand for electricity and hence a feed-back in direct demand for coal (which uses more electricity, and so on in a converging sequence).[1]

The uses of the general solution or inverse will be examined in the next chapter. In the rest of this section, the solution of the levels of industrial output required to satisfy any specific final bill of goods may as readily be calculated from equations 5 as from equations 6.

Some notable uses of the open model have been in analysis of the resource requirements of industrial mobilisation and of economic development. Suppose, for example, that the government of our imaginary four-industry economy anticipates a state of military emergency and draws up a bill of goods which includes civilian consumption, basic investment, essential exports and the manpower and material requirements of the armed forces. If we imagine the bill of goods was for four units each of wheat, flour, coal and electricity, then from equations (5) or (6) we can calculate the implied levels of output of these industries as 204, 4, 137·5 and 244·7 respectively. By applying to these figures the labour coefficients from the previous section, we find the total labour required by this bill of goods to be 23,065 men. Since this exceeds the work force of 20,000 men (from which anyhow must be deducted the armed forces' direct requirements of men in uniform), the bill of goods is not feasible and must be revised. In summary, the procedure is to solve equations (5) for the levels of output required to satisfy a specific bill of goods and then to calculate the implied demand for resources. This is then tested for feasibility against the resource supply.

In the above calculation the size of the work force was a limit to productive capacity. But other limits to productive capacity may exist, whether they be machine tool capacity or import capacity. The open model may be applied to these cases in similar fashion to that of labour, provided the necessary data are available.

For example, rapidly developing nations are often concerned whether their development plans imply a level of imports above that

---

[1] Such relations of circular interdependence are particularly noteworthy for the fuel and power, packaging materials and transportation industries which purchase inputs from industries to whom they sell. These loops of interdepend-ence may of course involve several industries as when industry i sells to industry j which sells to industry k which in turn sells to i.

which can be financed from export receipts and foreign loans. Once again then if the bill of goods (including exports) for the target year is drawn up and the best available estimates are made of input and import coefficients, the set of equations of the form of equations (5) can be solved for the implied levels of output. If the import coefficients are multiplied by these levels of output (just as the employment coefficients were previously multiplied by outputs) then the total imports are estimated and by pricing these we can observe whether they exceed the constraint set by expected foreign exchange receipts from exports and loans (which is analogous to the work force constraint). If the demand for imports does exceed this constraint then the development plan must be modified. This desire to anticipate balance of payments problems has been a major motive in the use of open models. While the open model is simple, its advocates point to its use as a method of avoiding bottlenecks by ensuring that the levels of output of industries are consistent with one another and with the available resources.

4. Prices

In our prototype three-industry model in section 1 above, the calculation of equilibrium prices is made by setting out for each industry its cost account stating that the value of output equals the sum of wage costs, costs of materials and other inputs and profit: Thus for industry 1 the cost account is

$$X_1 P_1 = (x_{21} P_2 + x_{31} P_3 + x_{n1} P_n)(1 + s_1),$$

where s_1 is the profit mark-up. By dividing this equation through by X_1, and performing similar operations on the cost accounts for the other industries we obtain the system of equations

$$\left.\begin{aligned}
\frac{1}{1+s_1} P_1 &= a_{21} P_2 + a_{31} P_3 + a_{n1} P_n, \\
\frac{1}{1+s_2} P_2 &= a_{12} P_1 + a_{32} P_3 + a_{n2} P_n, \\
\frac{1}{1+s_3} P_3 &= a_{13} P_1 + a_{23} P_2 + a_{n3} P_n.
\end{aligned}\right\} \qquad (7)$$

By substituting the known data on technology and profit rates this set of equations can be solved to give equilibrium commodity prices in wage-units. Thus in the four-industry example in section 2 above, prices were obtained by solving the cost accounts,

$$
\left.
\begin{aligned}
\tfrac{5}{6}P_w &= 100, \\
\tfrac{5}{6}P_f &= 200 + 50P_w + 20P_c + 60P_e, \\
\tfrac{5}{6}P_c &= 10, \\
\tfrac{5}{6}P_e &= 2 \qquad\quad + 0\cdot5P_c,
\end{aligned}
\right\}
\tag{8}
$$

to obtain the prices 120, 8,419, 12, 9·6 wage-units for wheat, flour, coal and electricity respectively.

The commodity prices generated by equations (8) are the total (direct and indirect) labour content weighted by profit rates.[1] In the case where all profit rates are zero, the price of any commodity in wage-units equals its total labour content (including both man-hours worked on-site and off-site in other industry producing materials used as inputs). Since there is a single scarce resource, constant scale returns and no joint production, it follows that there is a technically most efficient method of producing any commodity, namely the method which requires the minimum amount (on-site and off-site) of the scarce factor labour. Moreover, if all profit rates are zero this most efficient method will automatically be adopted under a procedure which costs all available methods of production and chooses that method with lowest unit cost. Somewhat less stringently, if all profit rates are *equal* and competing materials pass through the same number of vertical production stages, such a costing procedure will again specify the most efficient method of producing a commodity.[2]

[1] Demand does not influence price although price may influence demand.

[2] It may be emphasized that under the conditions just assumed, the technically most efficient method of producing a commodity is necessarily independent of changes in demand. In a zero (or uniform) profit state we reach the conclusion that a given state of technical knowledge implies that inputs be used in fixed proportions in producing a commodity. Thus if labour were the sole resource, changes in input ratios would result solely from change in technical knowledge and not at all from change in composition of demand. See P. A. Samuelson, *Activity Analysis of Production and Allocation*, (ed.) T. C. Koopmans, Cowles Monograph No. 13, 1951.

3

APPLICATION

1. The transactions table

Although the many-industry model of the economy so far presented is simple, this apparatus is used in problems of industrial mobilization and of economic development. This chapter considers in more detail the collection and use of data for such empirical enquiries.

The primary data collection problem is to assemble information regarding the nature of industrial technology. This may in principle be done either by directly ascertaining technical input coefficients from the industries concerned or by using a transactions table compiled for some past year as a source of data. (See table 1, p. 2.) Transactions tables are commonly used because they provide data which are consistent (in an accounting sense) and comprehensive. The two most obvious disadvantages of transactions tables is that they are likely to be at least partly out of date and that the *purchases* of a particular input by an industry during a period do not necessarily equal the industry's *use* of the input, i.e. transactions tables are an imperfect source of information on technical input coefficients because an industry's stocks of its inputs may change. But a more fundamental problem is that the output of a specific industrial sector in a transactions table represents a particular product mix (or ratio of the outputs classed together) and if this changes then the input coefficients may change—this is a problem to which we return below.

Let us then consider the procedure in compiling a transactions table (whether for economic analysis or to ensure that official statistics are internally consistent). The initial move is to compile two classifications, one of commodities and another of industries (or industrial processes) and to group all statistics on this basis. Investigators may wish to collect information on the quantity as well as the value of transactions—the quantity is used for technical coefficients and the value is used to check the accounting consistency of the data—and since most industries produce many commodities this means that

19

the number of commodities exceeds the number of industries. Since, moreover, some commodities are produced by more than one industry, we need an assignment table in addition to the transactions table so that the equality of total supplies and sales of a commodity may be checked, as well as enabling a check of the equality of an industry's costs to the total value of the commodities it produces. Such a pair of tables is shown in table 2 to which the following discussion refers.[1]

The compilation procedure now set out is dominated by the need to ensure that the information in the table is consistent and comprehensive. If, for example, there is a census of manufactures showing the total costs of each manufacturing industry in the classification, then these figures will be entered in the 'total costs' row (see table 2). However, even if these figures can be checked (for example by comparing data in the census of manufactures and the population census) these total cost figures are provisional.

The next step is to compile a provisional list of the aggregate supply of each commodity which is recorded in the right-hand column of the assignment table (table 2). Since records of commodity production are typically incomplete, the attempt is then made to assign the whole of home production to the producing industries back along the rows of the assignment table. The total of such commodity assignments to any one industry—obtained by summing the column for that industry in the assignment table—is the total recorded value of commodities produced by the industry. This column total in the assignment table can be checked against the column total for the total cost of the industry previously recorded in the transaction table. If the two figures are not equal an adjustment is necessary—which usually means that recorded production of commodities must be written up.

In this way firm control figures are established for total costs of industries and total production of commodities. The procedure is

[1] If a large transactions table with more than a hundred industrial sectors is consolidated down to around 20 sectors, we find it is substantially true that each commodity is produced by only one sector so that for some purposes it may be convenient to square the table by defining commodity i as the product of industry i. This was done for table 1 (p. 2). The procedure is illustrated by table 3 which is aggregated from table 2.

TABLE 2. *Lay-out for compilation*

ASSIGNMENT TABLE

£m. Commodity	Producing industry... a	b	c	d	Total output	Imports	Total supplies
I	3	20			23	2	25
II		4			4	—	4
III	23				23	1	24
IV			5	10	15	—	15
V				18	18	6	24
Σ*	26	24	5	28		9*	

TRANSACTIONS TABLE

£m. Commodity	Purchasing industry... a	b	c	d	Final home demand	Exports	Total sales
I	3	1	2	4	10	5	25
II	2	—	1	1	—	—	4
III	—	—	—	5	17	2	24
IV	—	2	—	4	9	—	15
V	1	4	—	—	19	—	24
Wages	16	13	2	9			40*
Profits	2	3	—	4			9*
Depreciation	2	1	—	1			4*
Total costs	26	24	5	28	55*	7*	

Industries are designated by letter, commodities by roman numeral.
Σ* Total value of commodities produced by each industry.
* Gross National Product (or National Income) (53) = Final home demand (55) + Exports (7) − Imports (9).

21

TABLE 3. *Aggregation into square*

Selling industry (product)	Purchasing industry		Final home demand	Exports	Total sales
	$a+b$	$c+d$			
$(a+b)$ (I, II, III)	6	13	27	7	53
$(c+d)$ (IV, V)	7	4	28	—	39
Wages	29	11			
Profits	5	4			
Depreciation	3	1			
	50	33			
Imports	3	6			
Total cost of supplies	53	39			

This table is obtained by aggregating the transactions table in table 2. After aggregation into this square form, since there is a one-one relation between commodities and industries, the table can be bordered by an imports row from the column in the assignment table. The layout thus obtained is similar to table 1.

identical for all industrial sectors although the information is often most difficult to obtain in the tertiary sector.

Now that the row and column totals have been established as consistent, the third step is to compile the main section of the transactions table either by searching for information on costs and inputs or by seeking information from producers on the distribution of their commodity sales among industries and final purchasers. The two approaches are complementary.[1]

The remaining important issue which has so far been postponed is the choice of the valuation basis to be used in constructing transactions tables. The choice of valuation basis is conditioned by three criteria: the need to balance the table in an accounting sense; the nature of the available statistics; and the objective of the compilation. As to the first of these, the need to achieve an accounting balance suggests that the table should be compiled either at producers' or purchasers' values. The difference between these two bases of valua-

---

[1] In finally achieving an accounting balance, the residual unidentified sales can be a problem. In general it is better to balance off those sales to the likely user (e.g. surplus timber is sold to the construction industry) than to sell to a dummy sector (which can distort results).

tion of a commodity is accounted for by transport costs, handling costs by the commerce industry (warehousing, wholesaling, retailing) and indirect taxes.

In terms of the criterion of available statistical sources, the choice of purchasers' values commends itself for two reasons. The first is that most purchases of materials by an industry are recorded on this basis, whereas little information is directly available on producers' values. The second is that the purchasers' value basis lends itself to recording entries in the *transportation and commerce rows* as 'handling charges on output' of the industry since the purchasers' values of sales of this industry to other sectors clearly comprises its internal cost structure plus handling charges on output. Now transportation charges for example, are typically available in the form of charges on output. By comparison the producers' value basis carries the implication that entries in the transportation and commerce rows must be the 'transport and commercial handling charges on inputs to the industry' since sales of this industry to other industries are on a factory door basis. But this sort of information is not readily available and can in fact only be obtained by an expensive procedure whose accuracy is open to doubt (e.g. to obtain the transport cost on all inputs into industry 1, distribute transport charges for each commodity along the commodity rows and then sum vertically down the column for industry 1).

In terms of the criterion of the aim of the compilation, if the aim is to collect data for use in an analytic model, the following two criticisms may be levelled at the use of the purchasers' basis of valuation: if a purchaser's value for an input is used to obtain an input coefficient, the implied assumption is not only that the material input coefficient is constant but also (more dubiously) that the transportation and handling charges on this input bear an unchanging proportion to output. Secondly, the assumption in the transportation and commerce rows that the handling coefficients on the output of industry are constant is of doubtful validity—compared with the assumption that the handling coefficients on inputs into an industry are constant—because handling coefficients on output are a function of the composition of the market, not a function of the particular industry's technology. These are valid criticisms, although the first does not apply if inputs are in physical terms, and as to the second, experience suggests that the rate of change in transportation technology is such that it is rarely wise to assume transportation coefficients of any sort to be constant. Instead, special studies of the transportation industry are needed.

The procedure for compilation of a transactions table has been detailed in order to give some insight into this important source of technical coefficients. Once the table has been compiled, input coefficients can be obtained by dividing the inputs into an industry by the level of output. The table of coefficients thus obtained may not only be used in an input-output model aimed at forecasting levels of output but may also be used to describe certain attributes of the economy for the year for which the table was compiled. These attributes are concerned with the factor content of final demand and we shall now illustrate this application.

2. Factor content of final demand

In equations (6) (chapter 2, p.15) we saw that a general solution or inverse may be calculated from the table of input and import coefficients. This inverse, together with factor input coefficients such as the employment coefficients (or import coefficients) for all industries, can be used to calculate the total, on-site plus off-site, labour content (or total import content) of any category of final demand D_i. All we need do is to decide the final demand or bill of goods $\sum_i D_i$ in which we are interested, solve equations (6) for levels of output of each industry, then multiply these by their respective factor input (e.g. labour or import) coefficients, and finally sum the result to obtain total content of the factor in the specified final demand $\sum_i D_i$.

This final demand might be: unit demand for one good such as clothing; or the observed demand in that year for a good or class of goods (say, rural products); or it may be some other classification of final demand such as the total export bill of goods. Since, moreover, we just noted that this information on factor content is calculated by industry, even more detailed questions may be answered such as: what was the level of employment in manufacturing industry sustained by all export demand; or what was the level of employment in

24

manufacturing industry sustained by export demand for *rural* products in the year for which the table was compiled? Each of these questions can be solved by a routine solution of the inverse for the specified final demands, and then multiplying the resulting levels of industrial output by factor input coefficients.

For example, the Australian transactions table for 1953–4 was compiled on a 40 sector (also a 20 sector) basis in financial terms so that the value of factor inputs into each industry were shown. Using as the unit of output of a commodity, the amount purchasable for £1 million in 1953–4, the table of input coefficients was calculated and then the inverse obtained. Then the export bill of goods for the year was substituted in the equivalent of equations (6), (chapter 2, p. 15), to obtain the *level of output of each industry* sustained by the export bill of goods. By grouping payments to Australian factors (i.e. wages, rents and profits, etc.) in each industry, an Australian factor input coefficient (contrasted with the import coefficient) was obtained for each industry. Multiplying these coefficients in turn by the levels of output just calculated gave the Australian factor contribution by industry to the whole export bill of goods. The result is shown in table 4 where the figures are condensed into four sectors.[1] The most noteworthy point here is that a large proportion of the value of exports is value produced in the transport and commerce sectors—a reflection of the fact that these two sectors employ one-quarter of the Australian work force.

TABLE 4. *Contribution by Australian factors by industry group to the export bill of goods in 1953–4*

Industry	Exports (£m.)	Australian factor contribution
Rural and food manufacture	701	450
Power, fuel, mining, engineering	99	100
Transport, commerce	—	188
Other industry	99	107
Import content		53
Total exports	898	898

[1] See B. Cameron, 'New Aspects of Australia's Industrial Structure', *Economic Record*, December 1958, p. 362.

By making this calculation not only for exports but also for consumption (public and private and including stock change) and for fixed capital investment (both public and private), and by separating wages from payments to other Australian factors (here referred to as 'other GNP content') we obtain the results in table 5. Other GNP content is high for exports because of the high rural land rent content. Other GNP content is higher for consumption than for investment both because of rural land rent as a cost component of food and clothing and because of indirect taxes on consumer goods (indirect taxes necessarily being included in the GNP content).

TABLE 5. *Factor content of final demand, 1953–4*

Aggregate final demand at market price	Value (£m.)	Import content (%)	Wage content (%)	Other GNP content (%)
Exports	898	5·9	33·9	60·2
Fixed Investment	1,137	19·7	48·5	31·8
Consumption	3,283	15·7	41·9	42·4

Further information is obtained by more detailed splitting of factor inputs. Thus if we let the final demand for coal be unity and all other final demands zero, we can calculate (see chapter 2, equations (6) p. 15) the level of output of each industry required to satisfy unit final demand for coal. By multiplying each such level of output by its factor input coefficients we can ascertain the total factor content of coal. This is an efficient procedure for answering the question: since the on-site costs of the coal industry include not only wages and profits but also materials, how may we decompose these materials costs into wages and profits to ascertain the total factor content of coal? The answer is shown for 1953–4 in table 6 for three chosen sectors: coal, iron and steel, and manufactured foodstuffs (not including beer and tobacco which have an abnormally high 44 % total net indirect tax content).

TABLE 6. *The average factor content of supplies of three commodities satisfying final demand. Australia, 1953–4 (per cent)*

	Coal		Iron and steel		Manufactured foodstuffs	
	*d		*d		*d	
Labour income	31	63	21	45	12	48
Mining rent	13	14	—	2		
Rural land rent					—	8
Depreciation	2	4	2	4	1	5
Interest, fixed capital	2	6	2	5	1	5
Margin	—	3	7	11	6	16
Indirect tax, net	2	5	2	5	3	6
Imports, c.i.f.	—	6	21	28	4	12
Commodity inputs	50	—	45	—	73	—
	100	100	100	100	100	100

*d this column shows only direct or on-site content.

3. An industry and its ultimate market

By using the approach set out in the preceding section, it is possible to ascertain the ultimate market for say, coal by calculating the proportion of total sales of coal which depend on the final demand for each commodity. Thus, in 1953–4, total Australian sales of black coal were £80m. (of which only £3m. were sold directly to final demand). By applying the final demand for gas and electricity to the inverse (see chapter 2, equations (6) p. 15) it was found that this demand supported black coal sales of £22m. throughout the economy. Similarly the final demand for building and construction was found to support black coal sales of £12m. and next on the list was the final demand for manufactured foodstuffs which, directly and indirectly, supported coal sales of £9m. So final demand for these products (representing one-quarter of total final demand) accounted directly and indirectly for more than one-half of the market for black coal.

A similar calculation performed for the iron and steel industry showed that out of total iron and steel sales of £90m. in 1953–4, two-thirds was supported by final demand for the output of the engineering, electrical, vehicle and construction industries. Rather

27

more surprisingly it was found that final demand for all rural products, foodstuffs and liquor supported £16m. of steel sales and that final demand for agricultural machinery supported a further £9m. steel sales. This meant that more than one-quarter of steel sales was dependent, directly and indirectly on the demand for the products of the rural sector and on the investment plans of that sector.

4. Imports

The manner in which imports are handled in an input-output model is of special importance if we are concerned with possible balance of payments problems. There are three basic ways in which imports have been treated and these may be described in terms of the way they appear in transactions tables such as that in table 1 (p. 2).

First, the bottom of the input-output table may be bordered by a row for competing imports and a row for non-competing imports as in table 1. The imports of commodity i shown in the cell in column i of the competing imports row are commodities competing with the produce of industry i—they are treated as inputs into industry i which are then re-sold to purchasers of commodity i. (In other words industry i includes the import agency for commodity i.) The non-competing imports shown in the cell in column i of the non-competing imports row are raw material inputs used in industry i, of a type not produced in the home country. A second and much more ambitious approach is to divide into two parts the entry in every cell in the first twenty rows of this input-output table: the two parts being the home-produced and imported purchases respectively. (This will henceforth be called a 'double-celled' table.) The relation between this and the first method is that: the competing import row is eliminated; the entry in column i in the old competing import row is dissected by purchaser and the figures thus obtained are subtracted from the original entries in row i, so that in each cell of row i there are two figures (for purchases of home-produced and imported goods respectively) whose value sums to the original figure in that cell. The second method then is a more accurate description of the actual course of events, since industries using imports of commodity i are no longer shown as buying these imports from industry i. The

28

bottom row for non-competing imports is common to both methods. The third method simply takes the layout obtained in the second method and sums all imports vertically in each column, and then uses each column sum to provide an imported inputs coefficient for the sector.

The second method, assuming its extensive data to be accurate, is the most searching of these approaches.[1] One may formulate a model to use the data, such as the following.

Output levels are determined by:

$$X_i = \sum_j a_{ij} X_j + D(h)_i.$$

Given these output levels, imports are determined by:

$$M_i = \sum_j m_{ij} X_j + D(m)_i,$$

where a_{ij} is the input coefficient of *home-produced* i into j; m_{ij} is the input coefficient of imported i into j; and $D(h)_i$, $D(m)_i$ are the final demand for home-produced and imported i respectively.

In addition, non-competing imports F are determined by

$$F = \sum_i f_i X_i + D(f),$$

where f_i is the non-competing imports input coefficient into industry i; and $D(f)$ is final demand for such imports.

Notwithstanding the advantages of the approach based on the double-celled table, it labours under the disadvantage that such data

---

[1] This form of input-output table is illuminating only because our classification of commodities groups non-homogeneous goods in the same commodity class. If a commodity class were truly homogeneous, this multiplication of detail in the input-output table would be superfluous: it would be sufficient to use an import coefficient which stated that say 20 % of commodity x is imported. It follows that the division of the cells of an input-output table into two parts is a device for solving an aggregation problem without increasing the number of sectors.

The matter may be summarized as follows. In a homogeneous commodity group a change in the import coefficient represents a supply oriented change, for example, the establishment of oil refineries alters the import coefficient for motor spirit. In a non-homogeneous commodity group a change in the group import coefficient may be the result of a *demand* oriented change, namely a change in the relative level of activity of industries purchasing different sub-commodities (having different import coefficients) within this commodity group. The double-celled input-output table provides data to analyse such a demand-oriented change.

are expensive to obtain and are available for only a few countries. Consider now, therefore, a fourth hybrid method which is relatively economical of data.

As our point of departure, consider table 1 in which all imports are shown in two bottom rows, one for competing, the other for non-competing imports. It is now proposed to distinguish three categories of imports in any cell i in the competing imports row: direct purchases by final demand; purchases by the industry i for its own use; and the residual which comprises purchases by all other industries j.

The justification for distinguishing imports of commodity i for use in sector i from other imports of i is based on two propositions. First, any industry which expands its output in order to substitute for imports is often likely to import more inputs slightly earlier in the productive process, e.g. the replacement of car imports by an expansion of car production may result in greater imports of electrical components, or an import-substituting expansion of cloth production may result in greater imports of yarn. Second, the crudeness of the commodity classification is often such that these products of successive processes—cars and parts, cloth and yarn—are included in the same commodity classification. Hence, if we are to understand what is happening to imports, say, in the textiles (yarn-cloth) group, it is desirable to distinguish the component commodities, since textile imports (i.e. yarn) bought by the textile industry may be rising while textile imports (i.e. cloth) bought by non-textile industries are falling.

The general ground for the proposed division of imports is as follows. If we look at the import entries along row i of a double-celled input-output table, consider what is likely to be the greatest source of aggregation error if these imports are summed to a single figure. In the absence of any other information about class i, it seems reasonable to suggest that purchases by final demand may be finished goods of a physically different type from intermediate purchases, while purchases by sector i are goods in process which may also be physically different from purchases of class i by other sectors j. Such physical difference is likely to be matched by a difference in import coefficients.

30

To implement this approach the basic equation to be used is:

$$X_i + M_i = \sum_j a_{ij} X_j + H_i + E_i, \qquad (1)$$

where X, M, H, E are output, imports, home final demand and exports respectively; a_{ij} is the input coefficient including all inputs i, *irrespective of origin*, used in industry j.

Non-competing imports are related to the output of the using industry by a technical input coefficient f_i. Hence

$$F = \sum_i f_i X_i + D(f), \qquad (2)$$

where F is total non-competing imports.

Intermediate demand for competing imports of commodity i comprises two categories: imports (M_{ii}) purchased by industry i and imports $(\hat{M}_i)$ purchased by all other industries j. The second of these $(\hat{M}_i)$ may be assumed to have a constant share of the market for sales of i to other industrial users, so that home production has the rest of the market and the two sources of supply are proportional, i.e.

$$\hat{M}_i = \hat{m}_i [X_i(1 - h_{ii}) - D(h)_i - E_i], \qquad (3)$$

where h_{ii} is the input coefficient for home produced internal sales of commodity i to industry i. The intermediate demand for imports by own industry (M_{ii}) may be assumed in general to be proportional to output

$$M_{ii} = m_{ii} X_i. \qquad (4)$$

Final home demand for home-produced output $D(h)_i$ is related to total home final demand (H_i) by the coefficient[1] m_{iy}

$$
\begin{aligned}
D(h)_i &= (1 - m_{iy}) H_i, \\
H_i &\equiv D(h)_i + D(m)_i .
\end{aligned}
\left.\vphantom{\begin{aligned} & \\ & \end{aligned}}\right\} \qquad (5)
$$

where

If exports are recorded net of re-exports, it may be appropriate to assume that no export demand directly requires competing imports. Since then

$$M_i = D(m)_i + \hat{M}_i + M_{ii}$$

---

[1] The status of the coefficients is as follows: f_i is a technical input coefficient; m_{iy} and $\hat{m}_i$ designate market shares; m_{ii} is a combination of technical and market share coefficient.

the foregoing equations (1) to (5) inclusive yield

$$[D(h)_i + E_i](1+\hat{m}_i) = (1+m_{ii}+\hat{m}_i - \hat{m}_i h_{ii})X_i - \sum_j a_{ij}X_j. \quad (6)$$

Equation (6) is a refined form of equations (5) (chapter 2, section 3, p.15), designed to permit more detailed analysis of imports for any given industrial classification.

5. Import substitution

From a set of figures such as those in table 7 one can conclude that if the ratio of imports to GNP had not fallen, imports in the second year would have been £400 m. It is tempting to interpret this as meaning that there has been import substitution measured by $(400-300 =)$ £100 m. 'import saving'.

TABLE 7.

Year	GNP (£m.)	Imports (£m.)	Ratio
1	1,000	200	·2
2	2,000	300	·15

That this is an error may be seen by recognising that if the composition of demand is changing, then the ratio of imports to GNP will fall or rise according to whether demand is rising relatively rapidly for commodities with low or high import content—and this without any change in the import content of any commodity. This suggests that no meaningful discussion of import substitution is possible unless aggregate demand is divided into commodity groups.

A straightforward method of analysing import substitution is to use the standard open input-output model[1]

$$X_i + M_i = \sum_j x_{ij} + H_i + E_i$$

in which

$$x_{ij} = a_{ij}X_j$$

$$M_i = k_i + m_i(X_i - E_i).$$

i.e. if $k_i = 0$

$$X_i + m_i(X_i - E_i) = \sum_j a_{ij}X_j + H_i + E_i. \quad (1)$$

[1] See B. Cameron 'Intersector Accounts, 1955–56', *Economic Record*, April 1960, p. 271.

The coefficients a_{ij} and m_i are available for 1953–4 from table 1 (p. 2). Suppose we then calculate production indices and import and export quantum indices for all commodity groups at constant prices for another year, 1957–8, for which year we then have a new set of import coefficients m_i'. Now we may ask: supposing that all import coefficients in 1953–4 had been those prevailing in 1957–8, with no other change in final demand or technology, what then would have been the level of imports in 1953–4? The answer to this enables us to attribute the observed change in actual imports between 1953–4 and 1957–8 first, to the change in import coefficients and secondly, to other influences—these two parts being numerically specified.

The above argument may be summarized: the analysis of import substitution at the aggregate level involves an 'aggregation error' and the way to handle this error is to use a multi-sectoral analysis. However a proper comment on this is that aggregation errors may always exist (even though they are reduced) for a classification of 20 or even 200 commodity groups. Hence there is a premium on minimizing aggregation error for any chosen commodity classification. Equation (6) at the end of the previous section (p. 32) provides such a means of reducing aggregation error.

By using this equation (6) instead of equation (1) above in an actual investigation into import substitution in Australia from 1953–4 to 1957–8, it was found that, had 1957–8 import coefficients (m_i') prevailed in 1953–4, imports in 1953–4 would have been £621m. instead of the actual £724m. Hence the conclusion was reached that during the four years ended June 1958, Australian imports would have risen £169m. ($= 18 \%$ of the rise in GNP) in the absence of any change in import coefficients—such a rise being caused mainly by change in the size and composition of final demand. Actual imports, however, rose £66m. at constant prices ($= 7 \%$ of the rise in GNP), the difference between the two figures being explained wholly by changes in import coefficients which were then analysed.[1]

1953–4 actual imports	£724m.
1953–4 [1957–8 m_i'] imports	£621m.
1957–8 actual imports	£790m.

[1] See B. Cameron, 'Import Substitution', *Economic Record*, December, 1964, p. 500.

33

6. Computation

When a system of linear equations (e.g. chapter 2, section 3, equations (5) p. 15) has to be solved for a specific bill of goods it is cheaper to calculate that particular solution rather than calculate an inverse (chapter 2, section 3, equations (6) p. 15). Particularly is this true if import coefficients are to be changed so that an inverse would not be used again. Hence we may briefly set out a convenient computing method to solve for the levels of output required to satisfy the specified final bill of goods.

There are two basic approaches to computing a solution. The first is iteration: the initial output of each sector is equated to final demand for its product and the implied intermediate demands are computed; then it is assumed that the output of each industry rises to match these derived demands and the next round of derived demands is computed; this process of converging on a solution is repeated. The second method is elimination, which is especially valuable if the equations can be ordered so that each output in any equation is dependent only on output levels in preceding equations.

The Gauss–Seidel method employs both these ideas. In the three industry equation system where final demands are (100, 50, 120)

$$100 = \quad X_1 \qquad -0\cdot5X_3$$
$$50 = -0\cdot2X_1+ \quad X_2$$
$$120 = -0\cdot1X_1-0\cdot3X_2+ \quad X_3$$

it is seen that the equations have been ordered so that, except for the entry in the northeast corner, each output in any equation is dependent only on output levels in preceding equations. This equation system is then nearly triangulated. Complete triangulation (i.e. all zeros above the principal diagonal) is not possible because of the loop or feed-back arising out of the fact that commodity 3 is an input into 1 and commodity 1 is an input into 3.

It is a feature of the Gauss–Seidel method that it uses the best available information at every point. Thus in the first iterative round the estimate for X_1 is final demand (100) plus use by industry 3, a total of 160. This figure is immediately used in estimating X_2 in the next line. Similarly when estimating X_3, the best available estimate of

34

First Round		Final demand	Intermediate demand	
X_1	=	100	+0·5(120)	= 160
X_2	=	50	+0·2(160)	= 82
X_3	=	120	+0·1(160)+0·3(82)	= 160·6

X_2 is 82 (not 50) and so this is used in the third line. The second round begins in the same fashion by taking the best estimate for X_3 from the first round. If we tabulate the results for the first four iterations we observe that they are converging rapidly because the sum of the column coefficients is much less than one. If we take the ratios of successive increments in these iterative solutions it appears that the increments form a geometric progression with a factor 0·08.

Second Round		Final demand	Intermediate demand	
X_1	=	100	+0·5(160·6)	= 180·3
X_2	=	50	+0·2(180·3)	= 86·06
X_3	=	120	+0·1(180·3)+0·3(86·06)	= 163·848

Using the formula for a geometric progression to infinity we can extrapolate the increment between the third and fourth iteration to find a value for X_1, i.e.

$$X_1 = 181·924 + \frac{(182·0539 - 181·924)}{1 - 0·08} = 182·065.$$

By similar calculation we obtain solutions for $X_2 = 86·413$ and $X_3 = 164·13$. Checking these solutions against precise solution by elimination, they are found to be correct.

Solutions in successive iterations				
	1st	2nd	3rd	4th
X_1	160	180·3	181·924	182·0539
X_2	82	86·06	86·3848	86·4108
X_3	160·6	163·848	164·1078	164·1286

In an industrialised economy, altering the order of the equations will not achieve complete triangulation because of the loops of interdependence between industries who, directly or indirectly, sell their products between one another. In practice at least 20 % of the volume of sales is likely to be left above the principal diagonal. Notwithstanding this, the Gauss–Seidel method is a fast efficient technique which was used for example in the analysis of import substitution in Australia set out in the previous section.[1] The method is of course applicable to other linear equations such as the set of cost accounts from which equilibrium relative prices may be calculated.

7. The aggregation problem

The need for input-output (i.e. multi-sectoral) analysis of the economy arises ultimately from the fact that demand for and output of different commodities changes non-proportionately. But this is a problem which we can never fully escape—like the index number problem, the aggregation problem is always with us and for the same reason, viz. non-proportional change.

The aggregation problem with respect to processes is the problem of ensuring that a column of input coefficients for an industry does not change because of a change in the relative size of the industrial processes which have (almost inevitably) been aggregated. However the conditions needed to satisfy this are stringent: the ratio of activity levels of any two aggregated processes must be constant either by chance or custom (as when the steel industry may expand proportionately the output of two different processes for producing steel) or because the whole of the output of one process is sold to the other process (as when all barley malt is sold to the brewing industry). Moreover the aggregation of commodities is only wholly acceptable if each user of the aggregated commodity purchases the component commodities in the same invariant proportion.[2]

The insidious nature of the aggregation problem may be illustrated by the writer's first input-output calculation in which it became apparent at the work-sheet stage that a rise in world demand for Australian wool was generating a rise in Australian imports of cotton. The explanation was rapidly found to lie in the nature of the

[1] For a fuller treatment of computing see W. Duane Evans, chapter 3 in *The Structural Interdependence of the Economy*, ed. T. Barna, Wiley and Sons, Milan, 1956 or to any text on linear computation.

[2] See H. Chenery, P. Clark and V. Cao-Pinna, *Structure of the Italian Economy*, Mutual Stabilization Agency, Rome, 1953, p. 35.

Australian aggregated textile industry: on the one hand some raw wool is scoured (classed as a manufacturing process) before export; on the other the cotton textile industry imports raw cotton; hence the aggregation of the textile industry irrespective of fibre meant that a rise in exports of scoured wool caused a rise in input and so imports of cotton. This problem is of course easily solved either by classing scouring as part of rural industry or by postulating that imports into the textile industry are a function of output *less* exports. But the more fundamental problem is to anticipate such absurdities arising at all.

Since the success of multi-sectoral analysis (with its claim to superiority over Keynesian aggregate models) rests largely on the success with which it minimises aggregation error, various attempts have been made to achieve this objective. One approach is to increase the number of sectors in order to escape aggregation error, but then to reduce the volume of calculation inherent in more detailed classifications by re-grouping industries into quasi-independent blocks. The principle involved here is that there are close connections between the several textile processes on the one hand and between the several heavy engineering processes on the other, but only tenuous connections between these two industrial groups which may therefore be regarded as quasi-independent.[1]

Another approach to minimizing aggregation error without causing too great a rise in volume of computation is to have a larger number of commodities than industries, the array of input coefficients thus being rectangular. This has real advantage if capacity limits for individual commodities are known. For example, in an iterative solution, if the capacity limit for steel tubes is reached, the import coefficient for tubes can be raised accordingly while import coefficients for other steel products are left unchanged. In this way a more realistic assessment is made of the amount of steel products to be supplied by home production.

[1] See A. Ghosh, 'Decomposition of the Technology Matrix into Quasi-independent Blocks', *Econometrica*, Vol. 28, January 1960.

8. Review

The investigator who seeks to move from aggregative models to multi-sectoral models of the economy has a variety of problems to meet, the most important of which have now been discussed. We can now, however, attempt a more complete review.

At the outset it is indispensable to formulate a closed aggregative (Keynesian) model to provide provisional control figures of demand and supply for a multi-sectoral model. These control figures are provisional because for example the forecast level of aggregate labour productivity is the base weighted sum of productivity in individual industries—but since the justification for input-output analysis is the prevalence of non-proportional change, it follows that base-year weights are wrong. In short, while the aggregative model is needed to provide guidelines, the multi-sectoral model will generate figures which should be fed back into a revision of the aggregative model. If in addition there is a systematic analysis of investment projects, then the analysis proceeds at three levels with a feedback involving each of them.

Since it is likely that the investigator will have to compile a transactions table as a source of data for his analysis he is involved in a number of initial decisions. First he must decide whether to collect information on transactions at purchaser's or producer's value or in quantities or both. Then he will aim at a classification of commodities and industries which hopefully will minimize aggregation error. Only then will he proceed to the chore of compilation.

Once equipped with a transactions table, another series of decisions has to be made if it is to be used to provide technical input coefficients. The entries in the transactions table are purchases rather than inputs; if the entries are in value they are costs not quantities, although one can regard them as quantities measured in a unit which is the amount purchasable for £1m. in that base year. Then one has to decide whether to net out internal sales in the principal diagonal i.e. whether to treat the output of an industry as the actual gross figure or net of its own use of the commodities it produces—for analytic purposes it is usually immaterial which basis is chosen so long as this is clearly stated.

38

A final decision is whether to manipulate the transactions table so as to have a rectangular or square array of technical input coefficients i.e. whether the number of industries and commodities is the same. One trivial point is that some statistical industries carry on technically separate activities—railway companies engage for example both in power generation and in real estate—and such activities can properly be hived off into their appropriate industry columns (i.e. a procedure of inter-column transfer in the transactions table). More important than this is the fact that many industries produce genuine joint products and as a further result some commodities will be found to be produced by more than one industry. Now there is no fundamental reason to try to suppress the fact of technical joint production; nor is there cause for theoretical concern in the existence of more than one source of supply since after all imports already constitute a second source of supply. Since the concept of a joint production coefficient is algebraically no different from an input coefficient, it is necessary to nominate the 'major product' of each industry and to describe the productive process as comprising not only negative input coefficients but also positive output (or joint production) coefficients.

4

TECHNOLOGY

1. Introduction

At any time, the technical knowledge available to an industry may be such that it can produce a commodity by several different processes each using different fixed equipment. Any such industrial process may be described by a production function stating the relation between the rates of input of measurable productive factors and the rate of output such that, given the state of technical knowledge and any technically fixed inputs, the function expresses the maximum product obtainable from any given combination of variable factors. The production function will show two characteristics of an industrial process which are of particular interest in the study of resource use, viz. the nature of scale returns when all variable inputs are increased in the same proportion, and the nature of opportunities for choice between inputs.

It may be emphasized that the businessman may have both a choice *between* alternative processes and a choice as to the ratio of inputs *within* a process. The discussion of choice within a process should not be allowed to obscure the fact that the choice between processes is not infrequently the more important.

In previous chapters we have used only the simplest type of production function characterized by constant scale returns and fixed proportions between inputs—and hence fixed technical input coefficients. We now examine other production functions with particular attention to opportunities for choice between inputs.

2. The production function

The two characteristics of a production function of particular interest are scale returns and opportunity for choice. While constant scale returns are undoubtedly common, we can readily imagine cases of diminishing scale returns (perhaps in the fishing industry) or increasing scale returns at least over a range.[1]

[1] For example, in the storage industry, storage capacity in a square building may increase with the cube of the side of the building but the input of materials used

Where a choice exists as to the ratio in which inputs are used in a process, the ratio chosen will depend on the marginal productivity of the respective factors as specified in the production[1] function. In theorizing on possible forms of the production function it is customary to postulate that the marginal productivity of any factor diminishes as its input increases, the input of other factors being unchanged. The justification for this is that under constant scale returns, increasing marginal productivity implies technical inefficiency.[2] For example, consider the output obtained from increasing the input of labour tilling a single acre of land, illustrated in the following imaginary figures:[3]

Labour input	Output (tons)	Rise in output
1	10	—
2	18	8
3	30	12

The factor-ratio in the second row is inefficient because it requires 2 labour units to produce 18 tons, whereas an equally weighted combination of the other two factor-ratios[4] will produce 20 tons from the same total input.

Various algebraic forms possess properties potentially suitable for describing a productive process. For example, consider

$$X = ax - b\frac{x^2}{y},$$

X being output, x and y inputs, a and b constants. This function is characterized by constant scale returns (e.g. doubling both inputs

in constructing storage may increase only with the square. A situation similar to this may prevail in the bulk transport industry, within limits.

[1] The marginal productivity of a factor is the rate at which output changes in relation to the input of that factor. The marginal product of a factor is the addition to total output from a (sufficiently small) unit increase in the input of the factor. The ratio chosen also depends of course on the prevailing prices of factors.

[2] In other words, increasing marginal productivity implies that output can be maintained (or increased) using fewer factors—which is inconsistent with the definition of a production function. (Increasing marginal productivity is equivalent to nonconvexity of the isoquant, discussed below.)

[3] The critical figure is 18. However, any figure greater than 10 and less than 20 will suffice instead.

[4] That is: the first factor-ratio is used to half-scale, one man working halftime on half an acre; and, the third factor-ratio is also used to half-scale, three men working halftime on the other half-acre.

causes output to double) and the marginal productivity of either factor diminishes as its input alone increases. A second example is

$$X = a\frac{x^2}{y} - b\frac{x^3}{y^2},$$

which is also characterized by constant scale returns and diminishing marginal productivity. Moreover, this function specifies that the ratio of input of the two factors must lie within the range

$$\frac{1}{2}\left(\frac{a}{b}\right) < \frac{x}{y} < \frac{2}{3}\left(\frac{a}{b}\right)$$

since outside these limits the marginal productivity of one factor is demonstrably negative.[1] A third example is the Cobb–Douglas production function

$$X = a.x^h.y^j,$$

which is also characterized by diminishing marginal productivity so long as the constant exponents h, j, are chosen as positive and less than unity.[2] If values of h, j are chosen so that their sum equals unity, then the function is characterized by constant scale returns; moreover, in that case the sum of the terms, factor input *times* marginal productivity, equals the level of production.[3] One attraction of this function to some writers has been that the elasticity of output with respect to the input of a factor is a constant whose value is the exponent of the factor.[4]

Whether any of these specific forms of the production function is useful in describing a productive process is ultimately an empirical

[1] $\dfrac{\partial X}{\partial x} = 2a.\dfrac{x}{y} - 3b\left(\dfrac{x}{y}\right)^2$, which $\gtreqless 0$ according as $\dfrac{2a}{3b} \gtreqless \dfrac{x}{y}$. Similarly for $\dfrac{\partial X}{\partial y}$.

[2] $\dfrac{\partial X}{\partial x} = \dfrac{h}{x}.X; \quad \dfrac{\partial^2 X}{\partial x^2} = \dfrac{h(h-1).X}{x^2}; \quad \dfrac{\partial^2 X}{\partial y\partial x} = \dfrac{h.j.X}{x.y}.$

i.e. if $0 < h < 1$, the marginal productivity of x is positive and diminishing as the input of x alone increases. Also, assuming $0 < j < 1$, the marginal productivity of x is increasing as the input of y alone increases.

[3] i.e. If $h+j = 1$, $\qquad \dfrac{\partial X}{\partial x}.x + \dfrac{\partial X}{\partial y}.y = hX+jX = X.$

[4] The elasticity of output with respect to the input of factor x is

$$\frac{\partial X}{\partial x} \div \frac{X}{x} = h.$$

question. There is, however, a general basic proposition which can be made under constant scale returns concerning the entire range of processes available to produce a commodity: the array of efficient activities for producing a commodity forms a convex set. This statement is explored in the next section.

3. Efficient activities

An activity or productive activity refers to a specific method of producing a commodity. Activities are assumed to be characterized by constant scale returns and to be independent of one another. An activity is defined by the column or list of input coefficients required to produce unit output of the commodity.[1] Any activity is thus characterized by a fixed set of factor proportions. Moreover, even if a process is accurately described by a continuous production function (with constant scale returns) we can furnish an alternative approximate description by listing a finite number of activities. For example, if there are three processes for producing steel and some inputs are continuously substitutable within each process, we may describe the relation between factor inputs and steel output in either of two ways: first, we may specify the three production functions; second, we may list a finite number of activities covering the operational range of factor proportions in all three processes. It is this second approach which is used in this book because choice between discrete activities appears to be characteristic of industry. This approach effectively bypasses the traditional production function by saying simply that a commodity can be produced by a finite number of activities, each of which is characterized by a specific set of input coefficients.

If there are seven known activities capable of producing a commodity, we may plot on a diagram the resources required to produce a unit of output by each activity. This has been done for activities A to G on figure 1. The activities A to E form a convex set and each of these activities is therefore said to be efficient. We can meaningfully join these points A to E since, for example, a point halfway along the line AB shows the combination of factors which would be required if half a unit of output were produced by activity A and half a unit by

[1] This definition can be extended to joint production by specifying unit output of one of the joint products, However, it is here assumed that there is no joint production.

43

activity B.[1] The uneven curve $ABCDE$ thus drawn is an isoquant curve showing all combinations of factors capable of efficiently producing the same (here, unit) amount of output. An isoquant curve can be drawn for any possible level of output.

It will be observed that the convexity criterion for efficiency involves more than comparing two activities to ensure that each uses less of some factor than the other activity. Such a comparison of two activities knocks out activity F (compared with B) but fails to knock

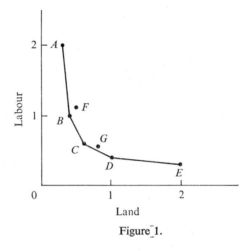

Figure 1.

out activity G. The criterion used here is that if there are three or more activities, it shall not be possible by a weighted combination of any two activities to produce the output with fewer factors than are used in any specified third activity. This knocks out activity G as inefficient since a weighted combination of C and D can produce the output with fewer productive factors. Expressed in a different form, the meaning of the convexity criterion of efficiency is that since there is a specified ratio of factor exchange between two activities, then for any third activity whose ratio of input coefficients lies between

[1] Under the assumptions of constant scale returns and independence of activities, the statement in text derives from the proposition: the weighted sum of the co-ordinates of any two points on a straight line, the weights summing to unity, gives the co-ordinates of a third point which is on that line.

them, the ratio of factor exchange must not be greater.[1] For example, we can switch from activity C to D by using two more units of land for each unit fall in labour input but to switch from activity C to G would require the use of four more units of land for each unit fall in labour input—more briefly the line CG is flatter than CD—so that activity is seen to be inefficient by comparison with C and D.

[1] The ratio of factor exchange—or technical marginal rate of substitution—is the extra amount of one resource needed to maintain constant output when the input of the other resource is cut by unity.

5

MAXIMUM PRODUCTION WITH TWO SCARCE RESOURCES

1. Introduction

Assume now that there are two resources, labour and land, and as before that there are constant scale returns, no joint production and productive activities are independent of one another. We wish to specify the maximum attainable national product, and in particular to examine the choice of methods of production since this choice is no longer merely one of minimizing total labour content per unit of output.

2. Choice of activities

Initially suppose that the equilibrium composition of final demand is known, an assumption which will be re-examined below. Then unit final demand can be visualized as a basket of goods in specified amounts. Suppose there are three commodities a, b, c—apples, beef, cotton—in the basket in the physical amounts 0·5, 0·3 and 0·2 respectively.[1] If it happened that there were just three efficient methods of producing each commodity, then there would be 27 combinations of these activities capable of producing the basket of goods; if two efficient activities for each good then there would be 8 combinations; and so on. In order to provide an arithmetic illustration of convenient size, we will assume that there are three efficient activities for producing good a, two efficient activities for producing good b and only one method of producing good c. These activities are specified in table 8 where negative signs designate inputs and positive signs outputs. We wish to ascertain what activities will produce maximum final output (i.e. maximum number of baskets) from the available resources.

Imagine that we arbitrarily choose an activity—say activity 1— for each of the three commodities. Then for that set of activities we can ascertain the total resources of land and labour required, directly and indirectly, to produce one basket of final output. This informa-

---

[1] Any physical amounts may be chosen.

tion is calculated in two stages: first, by solving for the level of output of each activity required to produce the goods in the basket;[1] secondly, multiplying those levels of output by the land and labour input coefficients. The result is shown in the first column of table 9 where combination (111) refers to the use of activity 1 for the goods (a, b, c) respectively.

TABLE 8. *Activities*

Commodity ...	a			b		c
Activity ...	1	2	3	1	2	1
Inputs *a*	+1	+1	+1	0	0	−0·4
Inputs *b*	−0·2	−0·2	−0·2	+1	+1	0
Inputs *c*	0	0	0	−0·1	−0·1	+1
Labour	−0·4	−0·2	−0·1	−0·5	−0·4	−0·2
Land	−0·1	−0·2	−0·5	−0·1	−0·2	−0·1

TABLE 9. *Activity combinations satisfying unit final aggregate demand*

Total resource input	Activity combination					
	111	211	311	121	221	321
Labour	0·497	0·377	0·318	0·455	0·335	0·276
Land	0·126	0·185	0·365	0·168	0·227	0·406

If this calculation is now done for each of the six possible combinations of activities, we have a list of the resources required to produce a basket satisfying final demand by any chosen set of activities. This is shown in table 9. These results are plotted in figure 2 as an isoquant map, where only the combinations forming a convex set need be considered.[2]

[1] The levels of output of the commodities, *a*, *b*, *c*, are here 0·597, 0·419, 0·242. In the present case, this is true not only for combination (111) but also for all other combinations.

[2] The fact that every efficient activity is part of a convex set (namely, the isoquant for a commodity) does not imply that all activity combinations form a convex set for the weighted basket of goods. On the contrary, while (111), (211) and (311) form a convex set, and (121), (221) and (321) form another convex set, these two sets overlap; if there were more methods of producing each com-

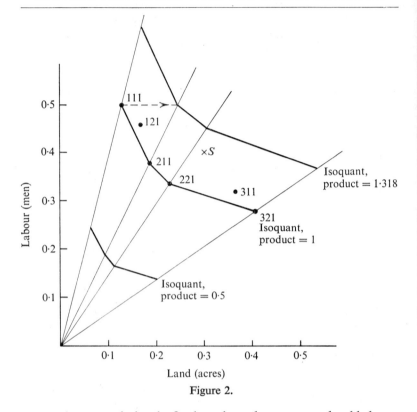

Figure 2.

In order to maximize the final product, the economy should choose from its efficient activities so that all available resources are used.[1] To illustrate the argument we will suppose that available resources are

modity we would find this overlapping to be systematic so that very many activity combinations are not in the convex set for the basket. However, an examination of the overlapping pattern indicates that no activity for a commodity is excluded from the convex set of activity combinations for a basket.

The explanation of the overlapping is seen readily from figure 2: if we wish to replace (111) by a less labour intensive combination, fewer resources are needed if activity $a1$ is partly replaced by activity $a2$ than if $b1$ is wholly replaced by $b2$ (where $b2$ means the second method of producing commodity b). Hence (121) is not part of the convex set for this basket; but this does not exclude $b2$ from the convex set for the basket and indeed this activity is in the final solution.

[1] This does not apply in the polar cases in which the ratio of resource supplies exceeds (or is less than) any attainable ratio of resource input coefficients. In these polar cases one of the resources is not scarce.

48

four million men and three million acres. Hence if it is proposed to use activity combination (111), this leaves large areas of land unused when all labour is employed; so more output can be produced by switching from (111) to the more land-intensive combination (211), thus enabling the economy to move out to a higher isoquant where with the same input of labour but more land, more final output is produced.[1] In short, since all activities are efficient, *the problem of maximizing national production is one of choosing a factor-use ratio equal to the factor-supply ratio*. It is possible to do this in four ways, some of which are based on placing activity combinations in an ordered sequence. The most obvious method of placing them in order is to construct an isoquant as in figure 2. A second method of obtaining an ordered sequence is to re-calculate the figures in table 9 to provide a marginal productivity schedule and then using a costing routine to knock out activities yielding a marginal product whose value is less than the price of the factor concerned. Two other methods of solving the maximum product problem which do not require an ordered sequence are: raising output by choosing better activity combinations until this process cannot be carried further; and minimizing the inputs required to produce given output.

These four methods of solution will be considered in turn:[2] the isoquant method is discussed first and the costing approach is left until last since it is basic to later chapters.

3. Ordering combination of activities

The simplest approach to solving for the optimal technology is to array all available activity combinations in order of rising ratio of resource input coefficients. The isoquant is such an array as shown in figure 2. In this diagram the point S, if joined to the origin, gives a line whose slope is the ratio of resource supplies. The straddling activity combinations (221) and (321) are those to be used. This illustrates the general proposition that if none of the activity combina-

---

[1] From the ratio of the labour input coefficients $0.497/0.377$, 31.8% more output is produced, as shown in figure 2.

[2] It may be noted that the solution procedures which use the opportunity cost concept will automatically knock out inefficient activities. Hence those procedures need not assume that the array of possible activities has been screened for non-convexity.

tions has a ratio of resource input coefficients equal to the ratio of resource supplies then, in order to use all available resources, we would use those two of the combinations of activities in the convex set whose resource input ratios straddle the ratio of resource supplies.[1] The chosen technology is then a weighted sum of these straddling activity combinations.

In the present example the solution is that 89 % of final demand will be produced by combination (221) and 11 % by activity combination (321).[2] In plainer language this means that commodity *b* will be produced by its second activity but that commodity *a* will be produced by both its second and third activities in the proportions 89:11. If the third method of producing commodity *a* were not introduced to this minor degree then some land would go unused. The maximum attainable national product is 12.17 million baskets.[3]

4. Achieving maximum output by raising output

This second method of specifying maximum national production starts from any arbitrarily chosen activity combination, and we then systematically investigate whether output can be increased by choosing alternative activities. To reduce the size of the calculations we will assume that combinations (121) and (311) have already been excluded.[4]

If we initially choose activity combination (211) from table 9, the maximum number of baskets producible (in millions) is

$$4/0.377 = 10.61,$$

[1] The maximum number of activities in the optimal technology equals the number of commodities plus $(n-1)$ where n is the number of scarce resources.
[2] The solution is obtained from

$$\frac{0.227h+0.406(1-h)}{0.335h+0.276(1-h)} = \frac{3}{4},$$

where h is the proportion of total demand to be met by activity combination (221). Here $h = 0.891377$.
[3] This solution is obtained from

$$0.335v+0.276w = 4,$$
$$0.227v+0.406w = 3,$$

where v and w are the scale of output of (221) and (321) respectively. $v = 10.8504$, $w = 1.3229$. Hence $v+w = 12.1733$.
[4] This does not limit the generality of the argument because the computing procedure knocks out all activities causing non-convexity.

and surplus land will be $3-(0.185 \times 10.61) = 1.037$ million acres. This is the first production 'Plan' in table 10.

In order to see whether output can be raised we shall regard activity (211) as embodying the only source of labour. Hence in compiling the first horizontal section of table 10 we obtain the input coefficients for activity combination (111) by writing an input of (211) amounting to $0.497/0.377 = 1.318$, since this input of (211) embodies the quantity of labour (viz. 0.497) required to produce a unit of output by combination (111). Since 1.318 of (211) also embodies $(1.318 \times 0.185=)\,0.2438$ land, we insert the land input coefficient $-0.1178\ (=0.126 - 0.2438)$ to show the additional (here, negative) input of land required. The input coefficients for the remaining columns are similarly calculated in the first horizontal section of table 10.

TABLE 10. *Ascertaining optimal programme by calculating cost of introducing new activity combinations*

Output and unused resources (million)		Input requirements per unit of output			
		(111)	(211)	(221)	(321)
1st Plan					
(211)	10·61	1·318	1	0·8886	0·7321
Land	1·037	−0·1178	0	0·0626	0·2706
Cost Z		1·318	1	0·8886	0·7321
2nd Plan					
(211)	7·8021	1·637	1	0·718	0
(321)	3·8355	−0·4356	0	0·232	1
Cost Z		1·2014	1	0·950	1
3rd Plan					
(221)	10·8504	2·2767	1·3906	1	0
(321)	1·3229	−0·9628	−0·3220	0	1
Cost Z		1·3139	1·0686	1	1

It is apparent from the calculations in the first horizontal section of table 10 that an additional basket can be produced by activity combination (321) *at the cost (Z) of a fall in production of 0.7321 baskets by combination (211)*. The introduction of (321) is seen from the Z row to produce a greater net rise in output than any other alternative.

51

Since we conclude that output can be raised above the level in the first Plan by introducing activity (321), we now ask what levels of output of activities (211) and (321) will exhaust available resources. The answer is (211) 7·8021 and (321) 3·8355.[1] This is the second Plan.

Once again, the task is to see whether this second Plan can be improved. For this purpose we need to calculate the input coefficients in the second horizontal section of table 10. This can be done for combination (221) as follows: since the sole source of labour and land are combinations (211) and (321), what reduction in the scale of these two combinations would release the 0·335 labour and 0·227 land needed to produce unit output by (221)? Since unit output from (211) absorbs 0·377 labour and 0·185 land, while unit output from (321) absorbs 0·276 labour and 0·406 land, the solution is given by

$$0{\cdot}377x + 0{\cdot}276y = 0{\cdot}335,$$
$$0{\cdot}185x + 0{\cdot}406y = 0{\cdot}227,$$

where $x = 0{\cdot}718$ is the required input of (211) and $y = 0{\cdot}232$ is the input of (321). The input coefficients in the column for (111) are similarly calculated.[2]

It follows from these calculations of inputs for the second Plan that an additional unit of output can be produced by (221) at the cost Z of a fall in production of 0·95. Since the Z row in the first Plan already suggested that (211) was more costly than (221), we drop combination (211) and draft a third Plan using activity combinations (221) and (321). The scale of these activities is calculated to exhaust resources and the testing procedure is repeated to see whether the third Plan can be improved upon. Since this is not the case, this Plan is optimal.

The third method of ascertaining maximum production is suggested by the fact that maximizing the output obtainable from available resources implies that resources per unit of output are being minimized. Thus if some arbitrary figure is assumed for national product (e.g. 10 million baskets) and if full employment of labour

---

[1] $0{\cdot}377h + 0{\cdot}276k = 4; 0{\cdot}185h + 0{\cdot}406k = 3$; where h, k are the levels of output of (211), (321).

[2] $$0{\cdot}377r + 0{\cdot}276t = 0{\cdot}497, \quad 0{\cdot}185r + 0{\cdot}406t = 0{\cdot}126,$$

where r, t are inputs of (211) and (321) respectively:

$$r = 1{\cdot}637, t = -0{\cdot}4356.$$

(4 million men) is assumed, we could calculate by an iterative procedure the activity combinations which will minimize the land used to produce that product. From figure 2—measuring both axes in units of 10 million—it is seen that these combinations are (111) and (211) and that less than 2 million acres is used. The national product can then be revised upwards and the calculation repeated until all available land is used. This procedure involves no new basic concepts and will not be pursued here.

5. Costing methods of production

This fourth approach to specifying maximum national production involves costing alternative methods of production using resource prices.

First, consider in principle how costing activities can specify maximum production. The convexity of the isoquant for the com-modity-basket reflects the fact that, as land intensity (i.e. the ratio of land to labour input coefficients) rises, the marginal productivity of land falls relatively to that of labour. The schedule in figure 3 is derived from table 9 and shows the marginal productivity of land falling as increasingly land intensive activity combinations are used.[1]

[1] The schedule is calculated from table 9 by re-stating the data for activities forming a convex set, assuming unit labour input.

Combination ...	111	211	221	321	421
Output	2·012	2·653	2·985	3·623	3·6375
Land input	0·254	0·491	0·678	1·471	1·500
Labour input	1·0	1·0	1·0	1·0	1·0
Output increment		0·641	0·332	0·638	0·0145
Land increment		0·237	0·187	0·793	0·029
Marginal productivity of land		2·705	1·775	0·805	0·500

The marginal productivity of land is then calculated as the ratio of output increment to land input increment.

If activities causing non-convexity are not initially screened out, they will be identified by the occurrence of increasing marginal productivity which indicates the existence of inefficient activities to be eliminated.

Since in practice there are very many activity combinations we must imagine the schedule to extend in both directions. For example, if there is an efficient activity combination (421) whose input coefficients in table 9 would be labour 0·2749, land 0·4124, then the schedule is extended as shown.

This schedule will now be read as showing the falling *value* of the marginal product of land for we will let the price of a basket be the *numéraire*. Like the isoquant, this schedule arrays activity combinations in an ordered sequence and we may proceed to specify the activity combinations consistent with maximum production in either

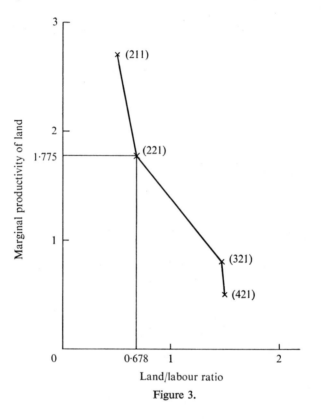

Figure 3.

of two ways. First, we may mark on the horizontal axis the land/labour supply ratio which is 0·75 and choose the activity combinations straddling that ratio. Second, we may place a ruler horizontally on figure 3 at a level representing any chosen land rent (e.g. a rent of 1·775 commodity price units); since no activity yielding a value of the marginal productivity of land less than this land rent will survive a costing analysis, we can read off from the schedule the land/labour

54

demand ratio at that land rent; plainly, we can lower the horizontal ruler until the land/labour demand ratio equals the supply ratio.[1]

In summary, the method of costing alternative efficient activity combinations is a workable approach to specifying maximum national production because there is a functional relation between the value of the marginal product of land and the land/labour ratio. Hence instead of the direct approach of choosing activity combinations whose factor input ratios straddle the factor supply ratio, we can use the method set out in this section which involves these steps:

1. choose an arbitrary land rent;

2. cost alternative methods of production using that rent, knowing that costing will knock out all land intensive activities yielding a value of the marginal product of land less than the land rent;[2]

3. ascertain the factor-use ratio (e.g. read it off figure 3) and compare it with the factor supply ratio to see if some available resources are unused;

4. if some resources are unused, revise the land rent and repeat the calculation.

Having established the reasoning underlying the costing approach to specifying maximum production, we wish to explore three topics: the direct application of this approach to the data in table 9 using the wage-unit as *numéraire*; the meaning of 'cost' in this analysis; and thirdly, in section 8 below, the possibility of considering this computing method as an analogue of real events.

It is seen from table 9 that if we initially suppose land rent to be zero, activity combination (321) will be used since it requires least labour, but at full employment of labour this would require

$$(4 \times 0.406 \div 0.276 = 5.9)$$

---

[1] Since the activity combinations are discrete, the equilibrium land rent moves discretely, e.g. having decided to lower the land rent below 1·775, we cannot stop at 1·7, but must jump down to 0·805 commodity units (= 0·33 wage units as discussed below). But in reality the activity combinations would be closely spaced.

[2] The choice of a land rent (measured in terms of the commodity price as *numéraire*) implies a specific wage rate (measured in the same unit). At the assumed land rent, costing will knock out not only excessively land intensive activities yielding a value of land marginal productivity less than the land rent, but also excessively labour intensive activities yielding a value of labour marginal productivity less than the wage-rate.

5·9 million acres; if we then raise the land rent to one wage-unit, table 9 shows (211) and (221) to be minimum cost combinations, and each implies excess land supply when labour is fully employed; by trial and error it can be found that at a land rent of 0·33 wage units, the minimum cost activities (221) and (321) leave neither excess demand or supply of land. This equilibrium land rent is not a market price but an imaginary or shadow price which we use to solve for the activities producing the maximum product of 12·17 million baskets.[1] This shadow price (of the use) of land equals the value of the marginal product of land in the optimal solution.

Having introduced the costing approach to specifying maximum national product, it is appropriate to consider the meaning of 'cost'. In chapter 2 where there was only one scarce resource, the price of a commodity equalled its total labour content (appropriately weighted by profit rates). It was thus possible, at least in the zero profit case, to regard the unit production cost of a commodity as the total resource content. Hence costing say a newly invented activity was an effective approach to ensuring maximum production, because if unit cost were higher than in currently used activities this must mean that the resource content of the new activity was excessive.[2]

This concept of unit production cost as total resource content no longer has meaning when there are two or more resources. If the costing procedure applied to potential activities is to make possible maximum production, then the price[3] of any resource must equal the value of its marginal product in the optimal solution. For this price measures the value of the loss of production if the supply of that resource were reduced by unit amount. Hence, if we proceed to cost a new proposed activity using such prices, we are measuring the loss of production involved in transferring resources from existing activities to the new proposed activity. This cost is the opportunity cost—i.e. the measure of production foregone by withdrawing resources from other activities—and it is the cost which is relevant to specifying maximum production. If this costing procedure yields a

---

[1] See section 6, p. 57, below for calculation.
[2] This statement is made with reservation about the effect of non-zero profit rates.
[3] Strictly we are talking about resource-use prices: land rent is the price of using land, not the price of the asset itself.

unit cost in excess of the existing price, this means that such a resource transfer would result in a net fall in production.[1]

6. The numerical solution

In section 3 above it was specified that the quantities of consumption of commodities (a, b, c) were $(0.5, 0.3, 0.2)$ respectively of the number of baskets of final demand.

Information on technology was given in table 8 and retabulated in table 9. It has now been shown that for the specified levels of available resources—4 million men and 3 million acres—the activity combinations in an optimal solution maximizing national product are (321) and (221), and that the shadow price of land use is one-third of a wage-unit.[2] Although profit rates have been implicitly assumed to be zero, the existence of uniform profit mark-ups will not affect the choice of method of production, although the distribution of the national income is affected.[3]

This array of information on resources, technology, degree of competition and demand enables a solution to be calculated for prices and production.

From the cost accounts

$$P_a = \quad 0.2P_b \quad +0.1P_n + 0.5P_t, \qquad (1)$$

$$P_b = \quad 0.1P_c + 0.4P_n + 0.2P_t, \qquad (2)$$

$$P_c = 0.4P_a \quad +0.2P_n + 0.1P_t, \qquad (3)$$

in which $P_n = 1$, $P_t = 0.33$, we calculate the prices of goods (a, b, c) to be $(0.3676, 0.5047, 0.3804)$ wage-units respectively, and the price of a basket is 0.41129 wage-units.

National income is $[4 + \frac{1}{3}(3) =] 5$ million wage units since full employment is assumed. The number of baskets satisfying final

[1] The costing approach set out in this section is operationally superior to the other three methods of specifying an optimal solution. They have disadvantages stemming from the number of homogeneous factors and the amount of computing involved in repeated matrix inversion.

[2] This is obtained by writing out the cost accounts for the two included methods of producing commodity a:

$$P_a = 0.2P_b + 0.2P_n + 0.2P_t, \quad P_a = 0.2P_b + 0.1P_n + 0.5P_t$$

yielding the solution $P_t = 0.33$ wage-units.

[3] 'Uniform' means that profit mark-ups are the same after taking into account any differences in the degree of vertical integration of industry which may affect alternatives.

demand is obtained by dividing the labour supply by the weighted labour input coefficient 0·328.[1] Dividing this into the 4 million labour supply we have 12·17 million baskets.[2] At a price of approximately 0·411 wage-units this is a *gross national product* of 5 million wage-units.

7. The role of demand

We may digress briefly to point out that while the composition of the final bill of goods was assumed given above, final purchasers have tastes which might be represented for example by the expenditure functions

$$C_a P_a = 0·446 \ Y, \quad C_b P_b = 0·369 \ Y, \quad C_c P_c = 0·185 \ Y.$$

These particular figures have been chosen because they would generate the numerical results already obtained.[3]

These demand functions play a role in determining both the shadow price of land and methods of production. For example, if tastes were to change so that a greater proportion of income is spent on land-intensive commodities, then land-rent will be forced up and some relatively land intensive activities may be costed out of production.[4]

It is salutary to keep in mind that demand functions play a role in determining shadow prices of factors:[5] first, because it may not be obvious in an open model that the specified composition of the bill

[1] From table 9 and from p. 50 footnote 2:
$$0·891377(0·335) + 0·108623(0·276) = 0·32859.$$

[2] The land input coefficients yield the same figure.

[3] If we postulate the expenditure function for commodity b
$$C_b P_b = k_b Y.$$
Then in the present case
$$C_b P_b = 0·3 \times 12·1733 \times 0·5047, \quad Y = 5.$$
Hence $\qquad\qquad\qquad k_b = 0·369.$

[4] For example, suppose that almost all expenditure is on commodity a, spending on b and c being negligible. Then from table 9 it will be found that the third activity for producing a will be costed out as too expensive.

[5] Opportunity for substitution in either tastes or technology can generate a positive land rent. That is, positive factor prices in an n-resource world may emerge either because consumers switch demand between commodities (of different factor intensity), or because producers can switch between methods of production (of different factor intensity).

of goods affects the shadow price; secondly, because if we specify a wrong[1] composition of the bill of goods we run the danger of specifying incorrect shadow prices and incorrect methods of production as well as incorrect levels of output.

8. Conclusion

Among the methods we have used to specify the optimal technology, the use of shadow prices as the basis for costing alternative activities is the most provocative. For it is easy to imagine that computing technique as an analogue of a real world in which maximum national product may be achieved not by central planning but by private businessmen bidding for scarce resources and choosing methods of production which minimize unit cost.

Let us then imagine a real economy in which decision-making is decentralized and consider under what conditions the activities of businessmen bidding for resources and costing alternative methods of production may be expected to result in the choice of technology which maximizes national product.

Now even in an economy in which there is no opportunity for choice between activities, the conditions for efficient operation of the economy include: adequate aggregate final demand; avoidance of bottlenecks; and the existence of adequate incentives for producers both to satisfy demand and to minimize unit cost by operating their plant without waste.

To these conditions for national efficiency we now add the following:

There should be no monopolistic restrictions whether in supply of resources, in access to methods of production, or in the supply of commodities which are inputs into other processes. Such restrictions are capable of altering the price system and thus causing a choice of non-optimal technology.

Further, factor prices should be flexible. The technique of costing alternative methods of production is not going to operate satisfactorily in a changing world if, for example, land rents are fixed by

---

[1] For the demand functions listed at the start of this section, a composition of the final bill of goods of (0·4, 0·5, 0·1) would be 'wrong' because at the commodity prices generated by the system, demand would not equal supply of individual commodities.

long-term contracts or the price of capital is maintained by institutional inertia or by financial mechanisms when these factors are no longer scarce.

This raises the minor issue that shadow prices have been measured in wage-units—so what happens when the ratio of the work force to land supply exceeds the most labour intensive method of production? The answer is that we may either use land-rent as *numéraire* and assign a zero value to the shadow price of labour, or we may assign some arbitrarily high figure to land rent measured in wage units. In either event we know that in reality this limiting case calls for the use of the most labour intensive methods of production and that the figure for land rent will be determined by social institutions. For practical purposes it is, in general, appropriate to use the wage-rate as *numéraire* not just because labour is a ubiquitous input but because it alone among productive factors will receive a price for its services irrespective of whether there is (open or disguised) unemployment of the factor.

The foregoing is not an exhaustive list of conditions to be satisfied by a decentralized economy if it is to achieve maximum production. Other issues crowd in, such as divergence between social and private costs. However in drawing up our basic framework of ideas it is perhaps more important to draw attention to two other matters which do *not* constitute limiting conditions to the attainment of maximum national product.

First, the fact that trade unions successfully demand a higher money wage-rate from time to time does not affect the argument. For in open competition it will pay producers to bid the price of non-labour factors (measured in wage-units) up to equal the value of their marginal product (in wage-units).

Second, it is not necessary to assume zero profit rates for the costing procedure to specify the optimal technology. It is only necessary that profit rates be uniform. For example, if there is only one vertical stage in the production of each final good and if the profit mark-up on each good is 100 %, then the optimal technology will still be chosen and maximum national production attained—though half the national income goes to profits—because the *relative* cost of alternative methods of producing a commodity is unchanged.

We should not conclude from this discussion that a decentralized economy will necessarily achieve maximum national production. Nor, incidentally, should we assume that central direction and decentralized decision-making can ever have precisely the same effects: central direction of an economy seems likely to be bureaucratic, cumbersome and derogatory of individual liberty; decentralized operation may involve privileged monopoly positions and excessive surplus productive capacity.

But it is reasonable to conclude that if the listed conditions are satisfied, then the use of ordinary costing techniques is likely to lead the economy towards maximum national production because the costs measure the loss of production in transferring resources from existing to proposed activities. Finally it will be noted that costing methods can as readily be used by planners as by entrepreneurs.

6

TASTES

1. Introduction

Throughout most of this book, it is assumed that commodities are consumed in fixed proportions. However, this chapter explores the individual's opportunities for choice—as contrasted with the business-man's opportunities for choice between productive activities.

The individual may exercise choice in either of two ways. In his capacity as custodian of resources he may choose whether to make these resources (his own labour-power for example) available to industry and if so, on what terms. The discussion of this topic includes the choice between work and leisure, as well as society's choice whether to reserve land for parks or to allow it to be used for urban development or cropping.

The second type of choice available to the individual, and the one explored in this chapter, is the choice between consumer goods which he can exercise as a consumer of final products. This choice is of fundamental importance. For so long as the same scarce resource is needed to produce two commodities, the consumer may switch between them in order to maximize his satisfaction obtained from a given group of physical resources—this substitution process is plainly comparable with the producer's switching between alternative activities to maximize the output of a specific commodity produced from given resources. Moreover, as noted in the previous chapter, either of these opportunities for substitution can account for the existence of positive factor prices—i.e. land (or any other resource) may have a positive rent: either because, as between two activities producing the same good, land has a positive marginal product; *or* because, as between two commodities with different factor input ratios, a positive land rent is needed to choke off demand for the land intensive commodity and thus establish market equilibrium.

The individual's choice between consumer goods is a reflection of his tastes and it is to a discussion of these that we now turn.

2. The description of tastes

There are, it seems, at least three general approaches to the description of tastes.

The first is the specification of a *utility function* showing an individual's total utility or satisfaction as a function of rates of consumption of all commodities. A property of this function is the marginal utility of any commodity x which is defined as the increase in total utility obtained from increasing consumption of x by one small physical unit, the intake of all other commodities being unchanged. We may then assert that the marginal utility of a good diminishes as the intake of the good increases, all other intakes remaining unchanged. The utility function is a non-operational concept of limited usefulness and the proposition that marginal utility diminishes as the intake increases merely reflects the adage that variety is the spice of life. Similar comments apply to the attempt to describe tastes by an *index function* in which, goods being capable of being arrayed *ordinally* according to rising satisfaction experienced, the index is a function of the rates of intake of all commodities.

The second approach is somewhat more behaviourist and is illustrated by the *substitution function*. This uses the concept of the marginal rate of substitution of commodity y for commodity x (briefly denoted as $mrs_{y/x}$) defined as the quantity of commodity y the individual is prepared to give in order to obtain an additional small unit of commodity x. Tastes are then described by the substitution function showing the marginal rate of substitution between any pair of commodities as a function of the rate of intake of all commodities. The proposition is then made that the $mrs_{y/x}$ diminishes as the intake of x increases, the rates of intake of all other commodities being unchanged. In summary, the description of the individual's tastes by stating the *mrs* between each pair of commodities as a function of his rates of intake has the virtue that it is cast in potentially operational terms: it is possible in principle to watch the individual's behaviour in the market in order to ascertain his marginal rates of substitution.

The third approach is wholly behaviourist and simply asserts that tastes may be described by market demand functions of the form:

quantity demanded of a commodity is a function of income, own price and prices of other consumer goods. Perhaps the best justification for this empiricism is that the other approaches tell us singularly little about the properties to be expected of such statistically specified market demand functions.

There is of course a formal relation between these approaches. Thus suppose we know the individual's tastes as described by the substitution function. Suppose too that the individual achieves maximum satisfaction which implies that he satisfies the condition that the *mrs* between any pair of commodities equals the reciprocal of their price ratio—

i.e. $\qquad mrs_{y/x} = \dfrac{P_x}{P_y}; \quad mrs_{z/x} = \dfrac{P_x}{P_z}; \quad mrs_{w/x} = \dfrac{P_{x_i}}{P_w}$, etc.—

for if he is not in that position he will gain by altering the *ratio* in which he demands commodities. Finally, the scale of his spending is limited by the budget constraint, i.e. if he spends all his income u

$$u = P_x . x + P_y . y + P_z . z + P_w . w,$$

where x, y, z, w are the quantities bought of those goods and the P are their prices. For any given set of prices and income, since the marginal rates of substitution are all functions of the rates of intake of goods, we may deduce the rates of intake or demand which satisfy the equilibrium conditions listed. (For example, for the four commodities x, y, z, w there are four equations to yield a solution for quantities demanded.) This may be done in principle for any set of prices and income and in this way the market demand functions derived from the substitution function. The importance of this imaginary exercise is its emphasis on the fact that market demand functions represent the end result of a search for maximum satisfaction by the consumer.[1]

3. Properties of the demand function

A property that we would expect to hold for any market demand function for a commodity is that quantity demanded remains unchanged when both money income and all commodity prices double.

[1] See H. Schultz, *Theory and Measurement of Demand*, University of Chicago Press, 1938; J. R. Hicks, *Value and Capital* (2nd ed.), Oxford, 1948.

However the response of quantity demanded to individual changes in income and price is varied.

Thus if money income rises, all prices being unchanged, real income has risen and the quantity demanded of a commodity will

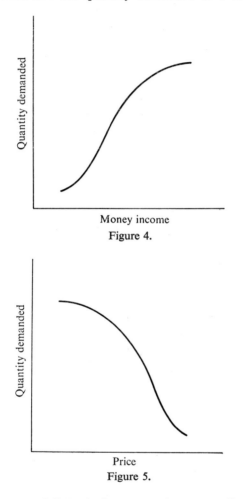

Figure 4.

Figure 5.

often rise but may fall. In the latter case the commodity is labelled an 'inferior good'. If the quantity rises as real income rises, then it seems likely that the demand schedule will flatten out as satiety is approached (figure 4).

If the price of a commodity falls, then not only has the individual's real income risen, but also the relative prices of commodities have changed. Hence demand is affected in two ways: there is a 'real income effect' and a 'substitution effect'. The substitution effect takes the form of an increase in the quantity demanded of the cheaper good.[1] But the income effect may stimulate either a rise or fall in quantity demanded: we must take refuge in the proposition that provided either an individual would buy more of a good if his money income alone rose or that the commodity is a minor item in the consumer's budget (so that any negative income effect is negligible), then a fall in price will result in a rise in the quantity of the commodity demanded. If the response to a price fall is a rise in demand, then the demand schedule is likely to be concave to the origin at low price levels (see upper section of figure 5) as satiety is reached, but at high prices the schedule may well be either convex or concave.

No useful generalization can be made about the effect of a fall in the price of *another* commodity on the quantity demanded of a good. For the goods may be competitive (butter and margarine) or complementary (gasoline and tyres) so that demand may rise or fall.

To what extent the demand function of a community of individuals with a specific income distribution may be characterized by properties suggested above, is a matter for statistical enquiry.

4. Market equilibrium

Some feeling for the role of demand can be gained by manipulating simple numerical examples. To illustrate, consider an imaginary isolated economy with 100,000 acres of arable land and a work force of 10,000 men available for employment. In the fishing industry the labour input coefficient is unity; and in the only other industry, wheat, the labour input coefficient is 0·1 and the land input coefficient is 2 (i.e. 2 acres needed to produce a hundredweight of wheat). This information can be plotted if need be to give a production possibility curve showing all attainable combinations of output—the curve ABC in figure 6.

---

[1] Assuming the individual to be in equilibrium before the fall in price of x, the price fall will stimulate him to buy more of it, thus reducing the $mrs_{x/y}$ until it is once again equal to the reciprocal of the price ratio. (Here y is any other commodity.)

If the demand for wheat is sufficiently strong then all land will be used in wheat production and output will be at B. The price of wheat moreover will depend on the strength of demand. Thus, if the demand functions were

$$C_w . P_w = 0{\cdot}9Y$$
$$C_f . P_f = 0{\cdot}1Y$$

Y is national income

C is quantity consumed

then with full employment of resources the equilibrium wheat price is 0·9 wage-units and land rent is 0·4 wage units per acre.[1]

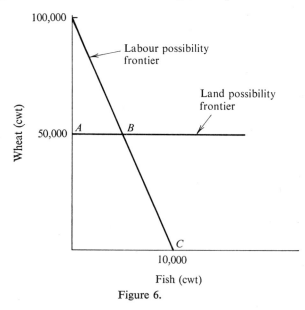

Figure 6.

However, if tastes changed so that only 80 % of income is spent on wheat and the remaining 20 % on fish then the equilibrium wheat price would fall to 0·4 wage units and land rent fall to 0·15 wage

---

[1] At full employment of land, 50,000 cwt of wheat is produced employing 5,000 men and leaving the other 5,000 men to produce 5,000 cwt of fish. Hence from the demand functions the ratio of wheat price to fish price is 0·9. Assuming zero profit rates the price of fish is 1 wage unit. Hence the price of wheat is 0·9 wage units. So the cost account for the wheat industry
$$P_w = 0{\cdot}1P_n + 2P_t,$$
where P_n, P_t are the wage rate and land rent respectively, yields a land rent of 0·4 wage units.

67

units per acre since the pressure of demand upon land resources is no longer so strong.

On the other hand, if in the original situation in which 90 % of income is spent on wheat, the work force were to rise to 15,000 through population growth, then the equilibrium price of wheat will rise to 1·8 wage units as the land rent rises to 0·85 wage units through pressure of demand on this increasingly scarce resource.

7

DEVELOPMENT

> If a country's population is growing at the rate of 1·5 % a year, and if again the capital coefficient is taken to be 4, then a savings rate of 6 % means stagnation, whereas a rate of 8 % means an increase in income *per capita* of 0·5 % annually.
>
> J. Tinbergen. *Design of Development*, p. 15

1. Introduction

In the last two chapters it was tacitly assumed that final demand comprised only consumption (private and public). The recognition of investment demand appears to introduce two problems for the investigator seeking to specify maximum production: how much to produce of investment goods; and how to allocate this production for use as between consumption and investment good industries. In fact, however, these are part of the same problem involving decisions as to the current level of consumption and future levels of consumption and production.

The more factors, both labour and equipment, that are allocated this year to the consumption goods industry (and the less to the investment goods industry) then the greater is the current output of consumption goods, the lower is the output of investment goods and the lower is a future level of production because less equipment will be available to raise output per worker. The decision whether to consume more or less now offers an opportunity for rational choice but it is a choice which is likely to be greatly affected by the State ideology, the inherited distribution of wealth[1] and by other institutions such as in the proportion of national income which is retained by corporate business as undistributed profits. This decision as to the allocation of resources between the consumption and investment industries is likely to be only peripherally influenced by the rate of interest and indeed in many economies the rate of interest probably plays a negligible role in influencing decisions to save.

After the decision has been made as to how to allocate resources

---

[1] Greater inequality of wealth often makes for a higher average propensity to save.

between the consumption good and investment good industries, the question later arises as to how to allocate the output of investment goods. This is the same question, but for the succeeding year. There is then a long-term decision at issue as to the growth path of the economy.

2. Development strategy

The quotation at the start of this chapter draws attention to the importance of the relation between the average propensity to save and the rate of growth of population and work force.[1]

To illustrate the issues involved in drafting a development strategy, let us consider the case where the country has such a low savings-income ratio relative to its given rate of population increase that it is able only to equip the growth in the work force with equipment appropriate to the inherited primitive technology. Failing gifts, loans, or costless improvements in resources or technology, to achieve a rise in living standards requires a rise in the equipment-labour ratio (as well as social changes including educational improvement), but this requires either a rise in the savings–income ratio or a fall in the rate of growth of population and work force. Several possibilities present themselves, of which the following is illustrative. If the rate of population growth is given, an appropriate strategy might involve these phases. In the first *revolutionary* phase, more or less painful methods (taxation, capital levy, forced saving by rentiers) may be used to bring about a progressive redistribution of incomes designed to make it politically and socially tolerable to hold aggregate national consumption constant in the face of rising population. This manoeuvre runs the risk of disincentive effects. The notable aspect of this phase is that since no rise in consumption occurs requiring new capacity, the output of the equipment industries may be allocated wholly to expand their own plant capacity[2] and this is continued so that the growth rate of output of equipment is accelerated by the strategy. Formally, we may summarize this phase by saying that the measures taken make possible a steady rise in the savings–income ratio, with the corollary of a higher growth rate of output of equip-

---

[1] The quotation assumes constant marginal returns to capital.
[2] Old equipment is also replaced however in both consumption and investment goods industries.

70

ment goods than of consumer goods. In time, however, efficient possibilities for income redistribution will be exhausted, and the first phase may give place to the second phase in which aggregate consumption is raised proportionately to population growth. Hence in this second *consolidation* phase, some of the output of equipment must be allocated to enable growth of output of consumer goods. However, it is an essential part of the strategy that, for the present, only the traditional primitive technology is used in the consumer industry because it is cheapest in terms of scarce equipment, and the first phase will have tended to create labour unemployment because of the high equipment–labour ratio in the equipment industry. The equipment required to raise consumption at the population growth rate using the traditional technology can be provided by the savings–income ratio at the starting date of the first phase. But the savings–income ratio has been steadily raised above that level throughout the first phase. It follows that during the second phase there continues to be an output of equipment 'surplus' to direct and indirect requirements for the growth of consumption. So the process of producing-equipment-to-produce-equipment, which was begun in the first phase will continue in the second phase. In summary, during the second phase the savings ratio will continue to rise, although less rapidly, and the output of equipment will rise at a faster rate than the output of consumer goods. At some stage, this second phase may be expected to give way to a third *bourgeois* phase in which the demands of households for higher *per capita* consumption cause the introduction at last of advanced consumer technology using higher equipment–labour ratios. This change, of course, is in conflict with the long-run objective of the strategy, in that it postpones the date on which the savings–income ratio will have been raised to the point at which not only the annual *growth* in the work force can be equipped at a higher equipment–labour ratio in consumer industry, but also the major technological conversion of re-equipping the entire *existing* work force at advanced technology can be begun. Indeed, if the short-run demands for higher living standards are sufficiently great, the growth of the consumer industry will directly and indirectly absorb the whole of the output of equipment, leaving no 'surplus' to continue the process of producing-equipment-to-produce-equipment. In that

71

TABLE 11. *Development strategy : resource allocation*

(All figures are in physical units)

| | | Labour | | | Equipment | |
| | | | Employment in | | Output of | Allocated for use next year to | |
	Year	Work Force Persons	Consumer industry $10(_1X_c)$	Equipment industry $1(_1X_e)$	equip-ment X_e	Consumer industry $1(\Delta_1X_c)$	Equipment industry $4(\Delta_1X_e)$
Stage zero							
2 % general	1	9,808	9,787	21	21·276	19·574	1·702
growth	2	10,004·16	9,982·74	21·42	21·701	19·965	1·736
	3	10,204·24	10,182·39	21·85	22·135	—	22·135
Stage one							
Consumption	4	10,408·32	10,182·39	27·669	27·669	—	27·669
constant	5	10,616·49	10,182·39	34·586	34·586	—	34·586
	6	10,828·82	10,182·39	43·233	43·233	20·365	22·868
Stage two							
Consumption	7	11,045·4	10,386·04	48·95	48·95	20·772	28·178
grows 2 % p.a.	8	11,266·31	10,593·76	55·995	55·995	21·188	34·807
	9	11,491·64	10,805·64	64·697	64·697	32·417	32·28
Stage three							
Consumption	10	11,721·47	11,129·81	72·767	72·767	33·389	39·378
grows 3 % p.a.	11	11,955·9	11,463·7	82·612	82·612	34·391	48·221
	12	12,195·02	11,807·61	94·667	94·667		

Inputs into consumption industry

$_1X_c$ is the output of consumer goods by activity 1, and for brevity only the input coefficients for this first activity are shown. The labour input coefficient for this activity is 10 so that the employment of labour in this activity $_1x_{nc} = 10_1X_c$. The level of output of this activity can be read from its employment column by dividing by 10, e.g. in the 7th year the output of consumer goods is 1,038·604 units.

The equipment input (or acceleration) coefficient for this activity is unity, so the allocation of equipment to this activity—$1(\Delta_1X_c)$—in the second last column is numerically equal to the rise in output of consumer goods in the next year.

Inputs into equipment industry.

$_1X_e$ is the output produced by the equipment industry by its first activity. The labour input coefficient for this activity is unity.

The equipment input coefficient for this activity is 4, so the allocation of equipment to this activity—$4(\Delta_1X_e)$—in the last column is numerically equal to four times the rise in equipment output in the next year.

event, the savings–income ratio would be constant at a point short of the objective. The political decision which specifies the rate of growth of consumption in phase three must then be consistent with the ultimate attainment of the fourth *modern* phase in which the equipment industry is large enough to enable technological conversion of nationwide industry to modern technology with higher equipment–labour ratios.

This strategy is illustrated by table 11. In the primitive stage 'zero' the work force is growing at 2 % p.a. and the equipment industry is just able to equip this growth of the work force at the traditional primitive technology. The output of consumption and investment goods are both growing at the same rate (2 % p.a.) reflecting a constant average propensity to save. Although only one method of production is shown for each commodity, the reader should assume that there are other efficient activities with rising equipment–labour ratios. The political objective is to achieve a long-term rise in living standards. This can be achieved only by moving to an advanced technology with a higher equipment–labour ratio and so higher output–labour ratio in the consumer-goods industry. Hence the need is to raise the output capacity of the equipment industry to such an extent that it will ultimately be possible both to equip the growth of the work force with an advanced technology and to progressively equip the *existing* work force with that advanced technology.

The stages through which the economy passes to attain this are shown in the table 11.[1] In the fourth year aggregate consumption is held constant, the decision having been made in the previous year[2] to allocate all equipment to expand the capacity of the equipment industry. (Some complementary unemployment develops in stage one because of the higher equipment/labour ratio in the equipment industry.) In the seventh year, consumption is allowed to grow at the same 2 % growth rate as work force. The essence of the entire strategy is that the level of consumption is specified so that its resource needs (especially of equipment) can be known and residual resources can be devoted to the expansion of the equipment in-

---

[1] Solely for simplicity in exposition it is assumed that replacement investment is zero and that it is the traditional equipment industry (not a more modern one with a higher equipment labour ratio) whose growth is to be accelerated.

[2] In effect equipment has a gestation period of one year.

dustry.[1] The equipment industry continues to grow more rapidly than the consumer goods industry, reflecting a continuing rise in the average propensity to save.

In stage three, aggregate consumption is to grow more rapidly than work force. In the ninth year it is found that a uniform growth rate of 4·83 % for both industries could be attained in the following year.[2] If the average propensity to save is to continue to rise, then the rate of growth of consumption must be kept below this. An annual growth rate of 3 % is chosen for aggregate consumption.[3] The output of equipment is growing at around 14 % annually. These growth rates are high relatively to the 2 % work force growth rate and are achieved only because there is unemployment. When full employment is reached some introduction of advanced consumer technology is necessary if consumption per head is to be raised: however, the extent to which part of the growth of the work force is equipped with the new consumer technology (and so the rate at which living standards can continue to be raised) must be limited by the need to ensure that the average propensity to save is still rising, i.e. production of equipment is rising faster than consumer goods. For in order to attain the long-run objective of higher living standards it is necessary to raise the capacity of the equipment industry to the point at which it can equip a uniform 2 % growth rate of the work force at advanced technology and still have surplus production to

[1] Thus in the sixth year the output of equipment is allocated for the next year initially to consumption industry 20·365 (= 1038·604 − 1018·239) leaving the balance 22·868 for the equipment industry. This will allow capacity output of the equipment industry to be raised by $\frac{1}{4}$(22·868) from 43·233 to 48·95 in the seventh year. (It is only in stage zero that the output of investment goods can be calculated from the uniform 2 % growth rate as

$$1X_e = 4(0\cdot02 \ _1X_e) + 1 \ (0\cdot02)_1X_c,$$

where $_1X_c$ is a datum.)

[2] Equipment needs are: $1.r(1,080\cdot564) + 4.r(64\cdot697)$, where r is the uniform growth rate. Since equipment supply is 64·697, it follows that r is 0·0483.

[3] The higher output of consumer goods is produced by the original technology (and not by an activity with a higher equipment–labour ratio) because there is surplus labour. The choice of the 3 % growth rate implies a rise in output of consumer goods of 32·417 (= 3 % of 1,080·564) in the 10th year. Hence in the 9th year, the allocation of equipment to the consumer industry—the acceleration coefficient being unity—is 32·417, leaving a residual 32·28 to be allocated to the equipment industry.

initiate and sustain the re-equipment of the bulk of the existing work force also at the advanced technology. This is a minimum condition for entering stage four in which the entire work force is steadily converted to a modern technology.

To illustrate, let us suppose that the second available activity to produce consumer goods has a labour input coefficient of 5. We wish to identify the size of the equipment coefficient which would be consistent with year thirteen being the first year of stage four.[1] In year thirteen, a 2 % growth of employment in consumer industry would be 236·15 which, with an input coefficient of 5 would produce 47·23 more units of consumer goods requiring an allocation of equipment of $_2b_{ec}$. (47·23) where this b coefficient is to be specified. In year twelve the output of the equipment industry is 94·667 of which 7·573 is needed to satisfy its own 2 % growth rate,[2] leaving 87·094 units of equipment for allocation to the consumer-goods industry. Hence the minimum condition for surplus equipment to be available to initiate the technological switch-over of the bulk of the work force is that

$$_2b_{ec}.(47·23) < 87·094,$$

i.e. $$_2b_{ec} < 1·844.$$

So for example if the equipment coefficient of the second consumer-good activity is 2, then the condition for entry into stage four is not yet satisfied.[3]

To sum up, two points may be emphasized which are relevant to any development strategy. First the levels of consumption must be specified at all times within a range which makes the objective of the strategy attainable.[4] Second, the level of consumption is numerically specified and other aspects of the strategy are contingent upon this, as discussed in the next section.

[1] The fact that there is still some unemployment is ignored in this illustrative calculation.

[2] $4 (0·02) (94·667) = 7·573$.

[3] Plainly the earlier introduction of the new consumer technology involves a higher need for equipment which will postpone the start of stage four.

[4] The treatment of investment in this chapter presumes that the target level of consumption is chosen sufficiently low to ensure that (more than) enough investment in extra plant capacity can be made to enable consumption demand to be satisfied. Hence there is no discussion of an equipment feasibility test, whether in the static form or in the dynamic form in which the test is actually part of the model (i.e. induced investment is determined by lagged acceleration coefficients).

3. Maximizing end-of-year equipment stock

In the previous section the nature of a development strategy was explored in order to indicate the issues involved in deciding upon the level of aggregate consumption.[1] Once a target figure has been indicated for the level of consumption for the ensuing year then, since the total available resources of labour and equipment (including newly produced equipment) are known, we may seek to specify the technology which will maximize the end-of-year stock of equipment. It is to be noted that this optimal technology refers to the activities used in both the equipment industry and the consumer-good industry.

The problem may be illustrated by an arithmetic example. The object is to produce 1 million baskets of consumer goods (of specified composition) and to maximize the end-of-year stock of equipment. The available resources are a work force of 4 million men and 5 million physical units of equipment. The alternative methods of production available for the consumer-goods industry are set out in table 12, and for the equipment industry in table 13.[2] All equipment is assumed to have a ten-year life and to depreciate by equal annual amounts.

Several methods of solution are possible. First, a listing of the alternative physical possibilities may be used as a basis for an intuitive solution. For example a sketch of the isoquants compared with available resources suggests that $3c$, the third method of producing consumer goods, might well be in the final solution. If this activity is used it will employ 2·5 million men and a stock of 2·5 million units of equipment, leaving a residual of 1·5 million men and 2·5 million equipment for employment in the equipment industry. This ratio (1·5:2·5) is very close to the ratio of input coefficients (2:3·5) in $3e$, the third method of producing equipment; and the adoption of this activity would produce 0·714 million units of equipment. It turns out by trial and error that if only one activity were to

---

[1] The composition of the final bill of consumer goods is assumed to be specified. The composition of the investment bill of goods is also separately specified.

[2] It is to be assumed that the data in these tables are obtained by a process detailed in chapter 5, section 2, i.e. matrix inversion, using the composition of the chosen basket, applying resource input coefficients, and eliminating inefficient activity combinations to make the set convex.

TABLE 12. *Consumer goods*

Resources required to produce 1 basket of consumer goods of specified composition by alternative activity combinations. (Physical units.)

Activity combination ...	(1)	(2)	(3)	(4)
Output	$_1X_c = 1$	$_2X_c = 1$	$_3X_c = 1$	$_4X_c = 1$
Inputs				
Labour	1·5	2·0	2·5	3·5
Equipment stock	4·0	3·0	2·5	2·0

TABLE 13. *Equipment*

Resources required to produce 1 basket of equipment of specified composition by alternative activity combinations. (Physical units.)

Activity combination ...	(1)	(2)	(3)	(4)
Output	$_1X_e = 1$	$_2X_e = 1$	$_3X_e = 1$	$_4X_e = 1$
Inputs				
Labour	0·5	1·0	2·0	6
Equipment stock	5·0	4·0	3·5	3

be used in each industry, then activities *3c* and *3e* would in fact maximize the end-of-year equipment stock. Two points, however, should be noted. First, the *use* of equipment (i.e. depreciation) throughout the economy is 0·5 million units (i.e. one-tenth of the stock in use) so that the net addition to the equipment stock is 0·214 million units. Second, the use of *3c* and *3e* leaves some labour unemployed (although not very much) so a better solution will exist which employs the entire labour force.

Taking up the suggestion in the last sentence, it is found that by using activities (*3c*, *3e* and *4e*) the net addition to the equipment stock is raised to 0·2167 million units.[1] But by using activities (*3c*, *4c*

---

[1] If *3c* is used, then residual resources available to equipment industry are 1·5 million men and 2·5 million equipment. If, where $k < 1$, 1·5 k million men are employed in activity *3e*, the complementary employment of equipment will be (3·5/2) (1·5 k) million, leaving residual equipment available to activity *4e* of [2·5 − (3·5/2) (1·5)k] million.

The employment of labour in *4e* will be 1·5(1−k) and the complementary employment of equipment is [3/6(1·5(1−k))]. If all resources are to be em-

and *3e*), the net addition is higher at 0·2222 million units of equipment.[1] It happens that this solution is optimal but not the only optimal solution.[2] This trial and error approach is unsystematic and is best regarded as a way of specifying approximate solutions as well as a way of suggesting an initial level of the interest rate to be used in the next approach.[3]

4. Shadow prices

A second method of solution is to specify an arbitrary figure for the rate of interest. The minimum cost activity for both consumer-goods and equipment is calculated. Then the resources used to produce the target figure for consumption can be calculated, leaving residual resources to produce equipment. This residual resource supply is then compared with the demand for resources by the equipment industry to see if all resources are employed. Two preliminary comments may be made before applying this approach.

First, the cost account for any commodity will include not only the cost of material inputs, wages and land rent but also two 'capital charges'. The first is the depreciation charge intended to indicate the amount of equipment 'used up'. For arithmetic convenience we are

ployed the two expressions in square brackets must be equal, i.e. $k = 0\cdot9333$. From this we can conclude that *3e* produces 0·7 million and *4e* produces 0·0167 million units of equipment, a gross total of 0·7167 million from which 0·5 million depreciation is to be deducted.

[1] If *3c* produces *h* million baskets and *4c* produces $(1-h)$ million baskets, then the residual resources available to the equipment industry are

$$(4-[2\cdot5h+3\cdot5(1-h)]) \quad \text{labour}$$
$$\text{and} \quad (5-[2\cdot5h+2(1-h)]) \quad \text{equipment};$$

and the ratio of these two terms should equal the ratio of the input coefficients in the equipment industry (2:3·5). Hence $h = 0\cdot944$, i.e. activity *3c* produces 94·4 % of the output of consumer goods. We then solve for the output of equipment.

[2] e.g. using (*3c, 4c* and *2e*), with *3c* producing 22·2 % of the output of consumer goods, is also optimal.

[3] The use of activities *3c, 4c* and *3e* is found, by writing out the cost accounts for the three activities to imply a rate of interest of 12·22 % per annum.

$$P_c = 2\cdot5+0\cdot25 \ P_e+2\cdot5 \ P_e.(r),$$
$$P_c = 3\cdot5+0\cdot2 \ \ P_e+2\cdot0 \ P_e.(r),$$
$$P_e = 2 \ \ +0\cdot35 \ P_e+3\cdot5 \ P_e.(r),$$

where P_c, P_e, r are the price of consumer-goods, of equipment and the rate of interest respectively. By solving this set, $r = 0\cdot122\dot2$.

assuming that all equipment has a ten-year life and depreciates by one-tenth of the original equipment in each year. The second is the charge for renting or hiring equipment for the year from society's scarce stock of equipment. This is similar to land rent and the symbol r designates this charge or interest rate.

Hence, if labour and equipment are the only inputs then the cost of production of consumer-good c by activity 1 is

$$_1X_c.P_c = {}_1x_{nc}.P_n + {}_1x_{ec}.\frac{P_e}{t} + {}_1x_{ec}.P_e.r,$$

i.e.

$$P_c = {}_1a_{nc}.P_n + {}_1a_{ec}.P_e\left(\frac{1}{t}+r\right), \tag{1}$$

where P_e is the price of a unit of equipment;

t is the length of life (10 years);

$_1x_{ec}$ is the volume of equipment used in producing commodity c by activity 1;

$_1a_{ec}$ is the volume of equipment used per unit of output of c by activity 1;

equipment is divisible.

Similarly the cost of production per unit of equipment e by its activity 1 is

$$P_e = {}_1a_{ne}.P_n + {}_1a_{ee}.P_e\left(\frac{1}{t}+r\right) \tag{2}$$

The second comment is concerned with the question whether the application of the costing procedure using hypothetical interest rates is in fact a method which will bring us to the objective of maximizing end-of-year stock of equipment. An intuitively affirmative answer can be seen from the fact that the depreciation charge prevents excessive use of highly productive short-lived capital equipment[1]

---

[1] If the cost account did not include a depreciation charge then the shadow price of capital would act as a rationing mechanism which maximizes *production*. This is similar to the problem in chapter 5 where production of good c was to be maximized—for 'land' read 'equipment'—except that now production of good e is being maximized after a specified amount of good c is produced.

But if length of equipment life is variable we may maximise production by excessive use of highly-productive but short-lived equipment. This is prevented by now introducing depreciation as an element in the cost account. In short the role of the depreciation charge in the cost account is to maximise end-of-year equipment stock when different sorts of equipment have a different length of life.

and the interest rate acts as a rationing device as did land-rent in chapter 5.

The basis for using hypothetical interest rates to specify the optimal technology, is laid by using the cost account for equipment (equation (2) above) to calculate the price of equipment produced by alternative activities at different interest rates (see table 14). Similarly, from equation (1) above, the price of consumer goods is calculated at different interest rates (see table 15).

At an interest rate of 12 % activities $3c$ and $2e$ are the cheapest in their respective industries. However if these activities are used we find that equipment is scarce (i.e. fully employed) and some labour is

TABLE 14. *Price of equipment at different interest rates* (r)

Activity:	$1e$ $(0 \leqslant r < 0.1)$	$2e$ $(0 \leqslant r < 0.15)$	$3e$ $(0 \leqslant r < 0.1857)$	$4e$ $(0 \leqslant r < 0.23)$
$r = 0$	1*	1·667	3·077	8·571
$r = 0.1$	—	5*	6·667	15
$r = 0.12$	—	8·333*	8·696	17·647
$r = 0.122$	—	8·929*	8·969	17·964
$r = 0.12\dot{2}$	—	8·999*	8·999*	17·999
$r = 0.123$	—	9·259	9·112*	18·127
$r = 0.13$	—	12·5	10·256*	19·355
$r = 0.14$	—	25	12·5*	21·429
$r = 0.15$	—	—	16*	24

* Least cost activity at the specified rate of interest.

The inequality at the head of each column is derived from the cost account and is a necessary (but not sufficient) condition for the activity to be used.

TABLE 15. *Price of consumer-goods at different interest rates* (r)

Activity:	$1c$	$2c$	$3c$	$4c$
$r = 0.1$	5·5	5*	5*	5·5
$r = 0.12$	8·833	7·533	7·083*	7·167
$r = 0.122$	9·429	7·947	7·456*	7·464
$r = 0.12\dot{2}$	9·499	7·999	7·499*	7·499*
$r = 0.123$	9·628	8·096	7·580	7·564*
$r = 0.13$	10·936	9·077	8·397	8·218*

* Least cost activity at specified interest rate.

unemployed. If we then raise the interest rate to 13 % activities *4c* and *3e* are the cheapest in their respective industries. However, although the use of these activities absorbs all the work force, some equipment is left idle so the rate of interest is too high.

The critical interest rate is 12·22 % at which level activities *3c* and *4c* are competitive, and activities *2e* and *3e* are also competitive. There is then no unique optimal solution but any optimal solution will comprise some or all of these activities. An optimal technology which gives an end-of-year equipment stock of 0·2222 million units may consist of: *2e* together with both *3c* and *4c*; or *3e* together with *3c* and *4c*; or of any intermediate combination.

Once again the most interesting aspect of this method of calculation is that it provides an analogue of how a market economy may operate. The rate of interest is raised until excessively equipment-intensive activities are costed out of production. Nor is the fact that the solution is not unique a cause for concern: it is not uncommon for alternative methods of production to co-exist competitively.

5. Conclusion

It has been implicity assumed above that equipment is non-specific. In reality resource allocation is constrained by the specificity of much equipment. This is not as great a restriction as might at first appear. For so long as the savings–income ratio is rising faster than the population growth rate, choice of technology is a one-way path towards activities with higher equipment–labour ratios. So long as all activities are efficient, the economy will move successively to more equipment–intensive activities and the entire problem of choice of technology really resolves into the timing of the introduction of new activities.

8

INTERNATIONAL TRADE

1. Introduction

Our initial premiss is that factors of production, in particular labour, are to some degree geographically immobile. If population settles in a region, whether it be Alaska or Australia, the labour force must work in order to survive. Given the tastes of the population, the question is whether world production and consumption is maximized by each region producing all the goods it consumes or by obtaining some of its consumer goods in exchange for exports of its own produce, i.e. by trade. To simplify the discussion, it is assumed that all commodities are consumer goods.[1]

For an imaginary isolated society which is opened up to possible trade by an enterprising naval officer or explorer, the proximate indication that trade is advantageous is a difference in relative prices of commodities at home and overseas, as here illustrated.[2] This

$ Prices in	Wheat	Beef
Country A	1	4
B	2	3

difference in relative prices must reflect some difference in the basic institutional data of the two societies (treating the rest of the world as one society). This may be a difference: in technology; in *relative* supply of measurable factors-of-production such as land and labour; in the quality of those measurable factors; in the distribution of such

---

[1] This chapter does not discuss influences affecting the location of industry within a region in which productive factors are highly mobile. Such influences are local variation in transfer costs and increasing returns to scale. For example it may pay to locate butter factories close to the raw material source (milk) because of weight loss in manufacture, but to locate bakeries close to the market because the product stales, and to locate fashion houses close to the market in order to keep in touch with changes in taste. Car production may be centralized in one big plant rather than decentralized smaller plants because of economies of scale.

[2] If all prices in one country are initially lower than overseas we may assume that the first flow of exports is paid for by a gold inflow which lifts the general price level so that the relatively dearer goods become absolutely more expensive at the given exchange rate.

natural resources as climate, soil fertility, accessibility and mineral deposits; or indeed in tastes or in distribution of monopoly power.[1]

In the historical development of ideas about the causes of trade, the first two of these causes have been given considerable emphasis. That is, emphasis has been given to the idea that differences in technology or differences in relative factor supply are causes of trade. Two comments seem appropriate on this. First, it is almost certainly true that many causes of trade are simultaneously operative for any community. Second, the basic data for an economy—its population, equipment, technical knowledge—are in a state of flux, and we would expect this to be reflected in changing patterns of trade.

2. The general equilibrium theory

The extension of the analysis to include interregional and international trade involves no really new principles. For each region or nation the basic institutional data to be specified are the factor supply functions, production functions, degree of competition and final demand functions. There is one superfluous (demand or supply) equation in respect of each region. There is a balance of payments equilibrium condition for each region save one. Also, the price of traded goods may not vary between regions by more than their transfer cost (including transport and tariffs) between the regions.

The problem is to see whether consumption is maximized by trading or not trading. The solution may be sought in more than one way. If the answer seems intuitively obvious we may postulate which region will produce which commodities, then calculate the implied solution, and finally test the validity of the initial hypothesis. Alternatively, we may use a hypothetical rate of exchange between the currencies of the two regions and shift this figure until we specify the solution in which each commodity is produced at minimum cost.

These two approaches will now be illustrated in turn by taking an imaginary case of two regions with different technologies—the Ricardian case.[2]

---

[1] If constant scale returns to scale do not prevail then the cause of price differences may simply be different size.

[2] D. Ricardo, *On the Principles of Political Economy and Taxation*, chapter 7 (vol. I, cf. *The Works and Correspondence of David Ricardo*, ed. Piero Sraffa, Cambridge University Press, 1951).

6-2

3. Two regions with different technologies: the Ricardian case

Our two regions are Queensland with a work force of 10,000 men and Victoria with a work force of 10,000 men, in each case labour being available for employment at any wage it can obtain.

There are three commodities, sugar, wheat and fish—the third of these not being traded because of prohibitive transport costs. Queensland is more efficient than Victoria in producing both sugar and wheat but is relatively more efficient in producing sugar: in Queensland, sugar production requires 0·5 men per ton, wheat requires 0·1 men per ton and fish requires 0·6 men per ton; in Victoria, sugar requires 2·0 men per ton of output, wheat requires 0·15 men per ton, and fish requires 0·6 men per ton. All figures are on an annual basis. Victoria also owns and mans the inter-regional transport system which has a labour input co-efficient of 0·0001 men per ton-mile. Labour is the only scarce resource and the industries use no other inputs.

The factory-door price of the product of each industry is fixed by applying a 20 % profit mark-up to unit cost (here, unit labour cost). However the transport industry makes no profit.

The consumption functions in Queensland are set out in a form showing expenditure on each good as determined by Queensland income and by the price of each good (expenditure, income and prices being each measured in Queensland wage-units):

$$^Q Cw.^Q Pw = 0·3 \ ^Q Y - 21{,}295 \ ^Q Pw,$$
$$^Q Cs.^Q Ps = 0·15 \ ^Q Y + 21{,}295 \ ^Q Pw,$$
$$^Q Cf.^Q Pf = 0·55 \ ^Q Y,$$

where Queensland's regional income $^Q Y$ is 1·2 times Queensland's wage bill.

The consumption functions in Victoria are

$$^V Cw.^V Pw = 0·2 \ ^V Y + 500 \ ^V Ps,$$
$$^V Cs.^V Ps = 0·3 \ ^V Y - 500 \ ^V Ps,$$
$$^V Cf.^V Pf = 0·5 \ ^V Y,$$

where Victoria's regional income $^V Y$ is 1·2 times Victoria's wage bill.

The final piece of information is that the distance between these two imaginary regions is 200 miles.

From an inspection of this array of information, certain conclusions seem intuitively reasonable. First, since the aggregate marginal propensity to consume is unity, there will be full employment in both regions. Second, the standard of living in Queensland will be higher than in Victoria which has a less efficient technology. Third, because there are relative differences in the technology of the two regions, the collective output of the two regions together could be raised by each specialising in the production of the commodity in which its relative advantage due to technical efficiency is greatest (or relative disadvantage least).

This latter point may be elaborated. An examination of the demand functions shows that: Queensland's demand for her own production of non-traded goods (fish) is constant at 9,167 tons (absorbing 5,500 men); and Victoria's consumption of fish is a constant 8,333 tons (absorbing 5,000 men). Hence the labour force available to produce traded goods (including the transport industry) is 4,500 men in Queensland and 5,000 men in Victoria. By inspection of the technical input co-efficients we find that these 4,500 men in Queensland can produce 9,000 tons of sugar or 45,000 tons of wheat or any combination in between described by the relation[1]

$$^QXs = 9,000 - 0 \cdot 2 \, ^QXw.$$

Similarly the 5,000 men in Victoria can produce 2,500 tons of sugar or 33,333 tons of wheat or any combination in between described by the relation
$$^VXs = 2,500 - 0 \cdot 075 \, ^VXw.$$

By summing these two relations

$$\Sigma Xs = 11,500 - 0 \cdot 2 \, ^QXw - 0 \cdot 075 \, ^VXw$$

we see that for any chosen level of total wheat production (ΣX_w), aggregate sugar production (ΣX_s) is maximized if Queensland produces as little wheat as possible. In particular, if the relative size of the regions and the nature of tastes is such that each region can

---

[1] ^QXs is Queensland production of sugar.
^VXs is Victorian production of sugar.
$$\Sigma Xs = {}^QXs + {}^VXs.$$
Similarly for production of wheat X_w.

produce sufficient to satisfy aggregate demand for a traded good, then *production of sugar will be maximized if Queensland produces no wheat*. It is this situation which is illustrated in the present arithmetic example. Collective consumption in the two regions together can be raised by Queensland producing sugar and importing all wheat consumed, while Victoria produces wheat and imports all sugar consumed.

By postulating that the two regions do specialize and trade in this way, we can calculate levels of production, trade and consumption which satisfy both the demand functions and the condition of balance of payments equilibrium.[1] As the calculations in the next section show, Queensland's labour force in traded-goods industry can produce 9,000 tons of sugar (of which she can consume 6,549 tons and export the remainder in exchange for 14,705 tons of imported Victorian wheat). Victoria can produce 31,427 tons of wheat (of which after exports, she can consume 16,722 tons). This is an aggregate level of production—i.e. 9,000 tons sugar plus 31,427 tons wheat—which is unattainable in the absence of trade as the technical input co-efficients show.[2]

An alternative procedure for specifying the solution under trade is to begin by postulating a hypothetical rate of exchange between the currencies of the two regions, use the cost accounts to specify which region produces each commodity more cheaply, test for balance of payments equilibrium, and finally repeat the procedure with a lower/ higher exchange rate if the balance of payments is in deficit/surplus. For example, let the currency in Queensland be dollars and in Victoria £; let the Queensland wage rate be $10 and the Victorian wage rate be £10. Then it is apparent that at a parity exchange rate of £1 for $1, Victoria would have a balance of payments deficit since all her goods would be too dear to sell in Queensland. We might begin by hypothecating an exchange rate of £1 for $0·6, which on being tested however will still be found to leave Victoria with a balance of

[1] For trade equilibrium to exist, the Victorian wage unit (measured in Queensland wage units) must lie within the range 0·25 to 0·66.

[2] For example if there is no trade: if Queensland produces 6,549 tons of sugar, she can only produce 12,750 wheat (with her 4,500 men in traded-goods industry); if Victoria produces 16,722 tons of wheat, she can only produce 1,246 tons of sugar.

payments deficit. The equilibrium exchange rate will be found to be £1 for $0·5.[1]

In summary, both computing procedures show that under free trade collective output is raised and that the increase in production is shared (rather unevenly) between the two regions. The advantage of trade to Queensland can be expressed in various ways: the increase in consumption of one good (Queensland gains by 1,955 tons of wheat); the opportunity cost of importing a ton of wheat at the equilibrium exchange rate which is 0·1667 tons of sugar requiring an input of 0·0834 men, compared with the 0·1 labour input coefficient for home produced wheat; or finally although Queensland is absolutely the most efficient producer of wheat, she is importing it for one-sixth the price of sugar, whereas to produce it herself would cost one-fifth the price of sugar. Victoria for her part is importing sugar at an opportunity cost of 0·9 men per ton—compared with her labour input coefficient of 2 for home produced sugar.

It should not be necessarily inferred however that free trade represents an optimum position for Queensland. The Queensland government might be able to turn the net terms of trade in her favour by appreciating her exchange rate to £1: $0·4 and restricting wheat imports by quota to equal in value the reduced value of her sugar exports.[2] The labour released from the sugar industry would be absorbed in the wheat industry. The loss implied by this labour transfer might be outweighed by the higher terms of trade. However, if Victoria can retaliate effectively then Queensland may finally be unable to raise her terms of trade and both regions lose through the reduction in trade and specialization.[3]

---

[1] Equivalently, from Queensland's point of view the price of foreign exchange (£) is 0·05 home wage units. At this level, exports equal imports at $14,705.

[2] A cruder method would be to tax sugar exports.

[3] Where more than two countries are involved, maximising the benefits from trade may require discrimination of a type equivalent to the effect of currency appreciation by a surplus country. See R. Frisch 'On the Need for Forecasting a Multilateral Balance of Payments', *American Economic Review*, September 1947, p. 535.

4. The Ricardian case: a numerical solution

Having postulated full employment and that Queensland will specialize on sugar production and Victoria on wheat production, the solution procedure falls into the following steps.

First, from the cost accounts we set out equilibrium prices, all prices (including the Victorian wage-rate) being expressed in Queensland wage-units:

$$^QPs = 0.6 \qquad\qquad ^{*V}Ps = 0.6 + 0.02\ ^VPn,$$
$$^QPf = 0.72 \qquad\qquad ^VPf = 0.72\ ^VPn,$$
$$^{*Q}Pw = (0.18 + 0.02)^V Pn \qquad ^VPw = 0.18\ ^VPn,$$

* These two prices are obtained by adding transport costs to unit cost at point of origin.

Second, by substituting these prices and regional incomes in the demand functions we obtain[1]

$$^QCw.^QPw = 3,600 - 4,259\ ^VPn,$$
$$^QCs.^QPs = 1,800 + 4,259\ ^VPn,$$
$$^VCw.^VPw = +300 + 2,410\ ^VPn,$$
$$^VCs.^VPs = -300 + 3,590\ ^VPn,$$

Third, by substituting the foregoing information into the condition for balance of payments equilibrium

$$^QCw.^QPw = {}^VCs.^QPs,$$

we can calculate the Victorian wage-rate which is consistent with the balance of payments equilibrium. This Victorian wage-rate is 0.5 Queensland wage-units, from which all commodity prices can be calculated in terms of the Queensland wage-unit.

It follows that Queensland consumption of sugar is 6,549 tons and of wheat is 14,705 tons, while Victoria's consumption of sugar is 2,451 tons and of wheat is 16,722 tons.

If the Queensland wage-unit is $10 and the Victorian wage unit is £10, the equilibrium exchange rate is £1—$0.5. At this rate, Queensland's wheat imports at $1 a ton c.i.f. cost $14,705; Victoria's imports of sugar at $6 a ton f.o.b. cost $14,705.

[1] The demand function for fish in each region is treated as redundant.

5. Two regions with different relative resource supplies: the Hecksher–Ohlin case

We turn now to consider another case in which the cause of trade is different relative supply of resources. This case was analysed by Hecksher and Ohlin and their main proposition may be stated: if two regions are similar save that their relative resource supplies differ, then the collective consumption of the two regions together can be maximized by each specializing on the production (both for home consumption and export) of goods having a relatively high content of its more plentiful factor of production.[1] For this proposition to be meaningful, we must add a restriction on the form of the production function: if commodity x is labour intensive compared with another commodity at one set of factor-price ratios, it must be labour intensive at all factor-price ratios,[2] and similarly for commodities which are intensive in other factors.

The theorem thus postulates that the collective output of two regions with different relative resource supplies can be increased by specialization, *notwithstanding that both regions have the same technology.* In order to explain this, let us consider an imaginary territory with a specified technology; the population have homogeneous tastes and indeed it will clarify the discussion to assume that all households at all times demand consumer goods in one specific proportion, so we may refer to a unit of consumer goods in this proportion as a 'basket'. The territory is now forcibly divided by a military commander into two non-trading regions, with one region being allocated more than half the land but the other region having

---

[1] B. Ohlin, *Interregional and International Trade*, Harvard University Press, 1933.

[2] James and I. F. Pearce 'The Factor Price Equalisation Myth', *Review of Economic Studies*, 1951–2. This restriction can be important. Even with identical functions for any commodity in all countries, an industry which is land or capital intensive in one country may be labour intensive in another. A. J. Brown, in his discussion of the Leontief paradox, explores the case where an agricultural product can be produced by a wide range of factor-ratios extending on either side of a narrower range of factor-ratios practicable for a manufactured product. The agricultural good may be labour intensive in the country with a relatively abundant labour supply but the manufactured product may be labour intensive in the other country. See A. J. Brown 'Professor Leontief and the Pattern of World Trade', *Yorkshire Bulletin of Economic and Social Research* vol. 9, no. 2, November 1957.

three-quarters of the population and labour force. If the Hecksher–Ohlin theorem is true, the military division will reduce the collective output of the two regions together; and of course by corollary either the reversal of the military division or the introduction of trade and specialization[1] make possible a rise in the collective output.

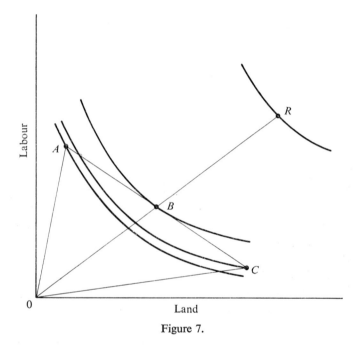

Figure 7.

The effect of the military division is to cause the region endowed with relatively more labour to shift to more labour intensive methods of production, and the other region will move to more land intensive methods of production. Thus each region adopts activities which are optimal for them in the new situation, but which were not optimal when the entire territory was not divided. The adoption of these new activities however implies a fall in the collective output of the two non-trading regions. The explanation of this lies in the convexity of the isoquant curve for the basket of consumer goods as illustrated in figure 7. Total resources of the territory are the coordinates of

[1] Trade may thus be regarded here as a substitute for migration.

point R, and before division of the territory the line OR measures maximum production. Assuming constant scale returns, then if the territory were divided into two regions with equal supplies of both resources, then each region would be a point B using the same labour/land ratio. However, the unequal division gives one region resources at point A, and the other resources at point C—so the first region adopts a more labour intensive method of production and the second adopts a land intensive method. Because the isoquants are convex there is plainly a loss of production, the size of which depends on the degree of convexity, i.e. the more shallow the curvature the less the loss.

6. Conclusion

The question asked at the start of this chapter was whether trade increases world production. Historically, a great deal of world trade in raw materials has come about because some regions have been unable to produce adequate supplies of certain commodities (such as tropical agricultural products, coal, iron ore) and have traded their own products in order to obtain these commodities. The more sophisticated arguments examined in this chapter go further to argue that countries collectively will gain by exporting commodities for which their costs are comparatively low—whether this lowness is due to better technology, relatively abundant factor supply or to other causes. Such arguments of course imply that a nation may with advantage import some commodities which it is well able to produce itself.

It does not follow, however, that trade is an unqualified advantage to an individual nation. There are several possible reasons for this. First, it is conceivable that a nation may invest in the establishment of export industries and then find the net terms of trade turned against her. Nations whose exports comprise a few major crops may find themselves in this position. Second, trade renders a nation susceptible to the depressions of other countries whose fall in demand for imports spreads depression to the export industries of all nations. It is clear that the government's task of maintaining full employment is made more difficult if the nations with whom she trades are themselves unsuccessful in preventing unemployment.

A third query, raised by Ohlin himself, is whether trade might benefit only one sector of the nation and might cause disadvantage to the rest of the nation. For example, in a land-plentiful country such as Australia, the introduction of trade causes rising export demand for land-intensive goods such as wool and wheat so that land rents rise; but imports consist of labour-intensive goods which compete with the produce of Australian labour and so the wage-rate may fall. If trade does disadvantage labour, measures may be taken to re-distribute income, though these measures may also effect output and trade.[1]

The fourth reservation concerning trade goes deeper. Some writers have pointed out that the relative cost advantage of a nation in producing a commodity may lie merely in that the country was first in the field. This leads to the proposition that a nation may set about altering its relative costs by conscious action affecting specific industries—whether this be in improved specialist educational facilities (chemical institutes), better transport facilities to mineral bearing regions (railways), or in willingness to undertake research and development in a highly advanced field (aircraft design). A more general version of this argument is attributable to Friedrich List (1840): that by encouraging the development of advanced manufacturing technology, greater demands are made upon the abilities of the population who respond by developing improved skills and knowledge and greater inventiveness.[2]

[1] For example, in Australia the method of redistribution chosen has not been a tax on the produce or incomes of exporters but an apparatus of tariffs on imports (combined in the past with a cost of living adjustment to the basic wage) which raises costs and so reduces the real incomes of exporters selling on the world market at a fixed world price.

[2] List himself had in mind the development of economies from a relatively primitive stage in which a predominantly rural economy makes fewer demands on the abilities of its citizens.

9

CONCLUSION

1. Review

Assuming demand to be adequate to sustain full employment of resources, and assuming levels of production to be so planned as to avoid bottlenecks in the inter-industry flow of commodities, we have considered the choice of methods of production consistent with the attainment of maximum production. (Though the problem was stated in this form, one might reasonably claim that the problem we were really seeking to solve was to maximize consumption.)

This analysis started (in chapter 4) from the concept of an efficient activity. Since the task is to choose from among methods of production, all of which are efficient,[1] it is necessary to adapt the choice of methods of production to the supply of resources in order to maximize production. So, if land is plentiful compared with labour, relatively land intensive methods of production are to be chosen.

The specification of these optimal methods of production can be done in various ways, one of which is costing methods of production with the aid of shadow prices of factors. This approach is effective because as the factor-use ratio rises, the value of the marginal product of the numerator factor falls. Hence, for any arbitrarily chosen factor price, the costing routine will knock out activities yielding a value of the marginal product of the factor less than the factor's price, i.e. a high land-rent will knock out very land intensive activities. So by revising the factor price up or down, we can adapt the factor-use ratio to the factor supply ratio.

When produced factors—equipment—are introduced into the discussion, the argument is the same. Where before a rent was put on the hiring of land, now a rate of interest is put on the hiring of equipment. In each case the task is to choose methods of production

---

[1] This slurs over the fact that convexity of the isoquant for each commodity does not imply convexity of the isoquant for a basket of these commodities. However, the point is of little significance since no efficient activity is excluded. (In any event, the methods of specifying optimal activities will all knock out any nonconvex activity.)

93

which imply a factor-use ratio equal to the factor-supply ratio. While the problem posed was to choose methods of production which would maximize end-of-year stock of equipment subject to a specified level of output for consumption, the problem could equally be regarded as maximizing consumption subject to satisfying the specific solution for the end-of-year stock.

Interregional trade offers a further opportunity for maximizing consumption and chapter 8 is an application to this topic of the concepts developed in the previous chapters.

It is irresistible to see in the calculations employing shadow prices, an analogue of the actual market place. The economy may indeed be regarded not only as a productive system whose output is a stream of final goods but also as a giant computer which generates a system of market prices. This giant computer takes account of more complex relationships—overhead costs, diminishing scale returns, taxes, tariffs, monopoly profits—than we have yet seen fit to introduce in our simple calculations.

So the investigator who seeks to specify the decisions as to resource allocation which will maximize production has himself a choice between elaborating a model capable of generating shadow prices or using the market prices generated by the economy.[1] The latter approach may, of course, be adjusted for taxes, tariffs, and monopoly profits,[2] as well as for notable discrepancies between social return and private return, i.e. the investigator uses 'quasi-market prices'. Whichever approach is used, resource allocation decisions are likely to be best made with the aid of a price system—ranging from the rudiments of 'costing' in this book to the discounted cash flow appraisal of investment projects.

2. Conclusion

The analysis in this book has been concerned only with exploring the implications of *specifying* a national objective such as maximizing production or consumption. Before one may examine how such objectives might in fact be reached, it is first necessary to describe

---

[1] W. F. Stolper, for example, favours the second alternative, cp., *Planning Without Facts*, Harvard University Press, 1966.

[2] M. Bruno, *Interdependence, Resource Use and Structural Change in Israel*, Bank of Israel, Jerusalem 1962, chapters 4 and 5.

the actual operation of the economy in terms of a set of lagged behaviour functions in market prices. Second, one must analyse the effects through time of the financial and other measures which may be used to attain the given real objectives. Such dynamic analysis is best undertaken against the institutional background of a specific society.

APPENDIX

DETERMINANTS AND MATRICES

The use of determinants and matrices reduces the work involved in solving large numbers of simultaneous linear equations. The notation is first explained below and then methods of solving equations are set out. For a full treatment the reader should refer to a standard text.

I. DETERMINANTS

1. Definition

A determinant is a square array in which each element must be capable of taking a single numerical value. A determinant of 2 rows and columns has four elements and is of the second order.

A determinant of the second order is defined as taking its value from the difference between the cross products of the four elements:

$$\begin{vmatrix} a_{11} & a_{12} \\ a_{21} & a_{22} \end{vmatrix} = a_{11}a_{22} - a_{12}a_{21}.$$

For example the following determinant is found to have the value 13.

$$\begin{vmatrix} 4 & -1 \\ 1 & 3 \end{vmatrix} = 13.$$

A determinant of the third order is defined in terms of those of the second order by the rule (signs alternating + and − as the sum of the subscripts of the underlined elements are even or odd):

$$\begin{vmatrix} a_{11} & a_{12} & a_{13} \\ a_{21} & a_{22} & a_{23} \\ a_{31} & a_{32} & a_{33} \end{vmatrix} = a_{11}\begin{vmatrix} a_{22} & a_{23} \\ a_{32} & a_{33} \end{vmatrix} - a_{12}\begin{vmatrix} a_{21} & a_{23} \\ a_{31} & a_{33} \end{vmatrix} + a_{13}\begin{vmatrix} a_{21} & a_{22} \\ a_{31} & a_{32} \end{vmatrix}$$

This is called an expansion of the third-order determinant. For example, we can expand

$$\begin{vmatrix} 1 & -1 & 0 \\ 4 & 5 & 3 \\ 2 & 0 & -6 \end{vmatrix} = 1\begin{vmatrix} 5 & 3 \\ 0 & -6 \end{vmatrix} - (-1)\begin{vmatrix} 4 & 3 \\ 2 & -6 \end{vmatrix} + 0\begin{vmatrix} 4 & 5 \\ 2 & 0 \end{vmatrix} = -60.$$

Determinants of higher order may be defined by an extension of the above method, as seen below.

2. Minors and co-factors

Selecting an element of a given determinant (say a_{13} above), delete the row and column intersecting in the element and thus obtain a determinant of order one less than that of the original determinant. The determinant thus obtained is called the *minor* of the selected element in the original determinant. The *co-factor* of the selected element is the minor with a sign attached (positive if subscripts of the selected element add to an even number, negative if odd).

It can now be seen that section 1 shows how to evaluate a third-order determinant by an expansion of signed minors (i.e. co-factors) of the first row. Indeed the reader can easily satisfy himself that the above determinants can be evaluated by an *expansion of signed minors of any row or column*—simply choose a row or column of elements, multiply each element by its minor (whose sign is determined by the sum of the subscripts), and sum the signed products.

3. Properties of determinants

(i) The multiplication of all the elements of a row or column by the same quantity, causes the value of the determinant to be multiplied by that quantity, e.g.:

$$\begin{vmatrix} 24 & 15 \\ 18 & 5 \end{vmatrix} = 6 \begin{vmatrix} 4 & 15 \\ 3 & 5 \end{vmatrix} = 6 \cdot 5 \begin{vmatrix} 4 & 3 \\ 3 & 1 \end{vmatrix} = -150.$$

(ii) A determinant with two identically matched rows (or columns) has the value zero.

This is obvious for the second-order determinant

$$\begin{vmatrix} x & x \\ y & y \end{vmatrix}.$$

The argument can readily be extended: in a third-order determinant whose second and third rows are identical, in an expansion by minors of the first row all minors have zero value. The argument can similarly be extended to higher orders.

By considering both the properties just listed, we note the corollary that if two rows (or columns) of a determinant are proportional, the determinant has zero value. (We can take the factor of proportionality to the outside without altering the value of the determinant, but this leaves identical rows.)

From these properties we now derive in the next two sections two propositions which will be used later.

4. Expansions in terms of alien co-factors vanish

With respect to the elements of a given row or column (e.g. the second row), the co-factors of elements in a different row or column (e.g. the first row) are called *alien* co-factors.

To illustrate, we write A_{11} as the symbol for the co-factor of the element a_{11}. So that the determinant

$$\begin{vmatrix} a_{11} & a_{12} & a_{13} \\ a_{21} & a_{22} & a_{23} \\ a_{31} & a_{32} & a_{33} \end{vmatrix} = a_{11} \begin{vmatrix} a_{22} & a_{23} \\ a_{32} & a_{33} \end{vmatrix} - a_{12} \begin{vmatrix} a_{21} & a_{23} \\ a_{31} & a_{33} \end{vmatrix} + a_{13} \begin{vmatrix} a_{21} & a_{22} \\ a_{31} & a_{32} \end{vmatrix}$$

$$= a_{11} A_{11} + a_{12} A_{12} + a_{13} A_{13}.$$

Now the following expression is an expansion in terms of alien co-factors (elements of second row but co-factors of first row) and since it has two identical rows, it has zero value. Hence expansions in terms of alien co-factors have zero value.

$$a_{21} A_{11} + a_{22} A_{12} + a_{23} A_{13} = \begin{vmatrix} a_{21} & a_{22} & a_{23} \\ a_{21} & a_{22} & a_{23} \\ a_{31} & a_{32} & a_{33} \end{vmatrix}.$$

5. Manipulating a determinant with constant value

We now wish to demonstrate this proposition which is helpful in calculating the value of determinants:

Let the elements of a row (or column) each be multiplied by the same quantity and then added to the corresponding elements of a second row (or column). Then the value of the determinant is unchanged.

Thus, consider the third-order determinant D

$$D = \begin{vmatrix} a_1 & b_1 & c_1 \\ a_2 & b_2 & c_2 \\ a_3 & b_3 & c_3 \end{vmatrix}.$$

Following the prescribed procedure we obtain the determinant Δ:

$$\Delta = \begin{vmatrix} a_1+kb_1 & b_1 & c_1 \\ a_2+kb_2 & b_2 & c_2 \\ a_3+kb_3 & b_3 & c_3 \end{vmatrix}.$$

Now a consideration of the nature of determinants—expand by elements of the first column—shows that Δ can be re-written as the sum of two determinants

$$\Delta = \begin{vmatrix} a_1 & b_1 & c_1 \\ a_2 & b_2 & c_2 \\ a_3 & b_3 & c_3 \end{vmatrix} + \begin{vmatrix} kb_1 & b_1 & c_1 \\ kb_2 & b_2 & c_2 \\ kb_3 & b_3 & c_3 \end{vmatrix}.$$

Since the last of these determinants has a zero value we conclude that $\Delta = D$.

The usefulness of this manipulation may be illustrated by evaluating

$$\begin{vmatrix} 6 & 3 & 9 & 4 \\ 8 & 2 & 7 & 5 \\ 5 & 4 & 3 & 0 \\ 1 & 3 & 6 & 2 \end{vmatrix}.$$

By multiplying the fourth row by 6 and subtracting from the first row, we obtain

$$\begin{vmatrix} 0 & -15 & -25 & -8 \\ 8 & 2 & 7 & 5 \\ 5 & 4 & 3 & 0 \\ 1 & 3 & 6 & 2 \end{vmatrix}.$$

By repeating this device the first three elements in the first column can be made zeros so that a third-order determinant of unchanged value is obtained. The determinant is found to have a value 364.

6. Cramer's rule

Cramer's rule states that the three simultaneous equations in 3 unknowns

$$\left.\begin{array}{l} a_1 x + b_1 y + c_1 z = k_1, \\ a_2 x + b_2 y + c_2 z = k_2, \\ a_3 x + b_3 y + c_3 z = k_3. \end{array}\right\} \qquad (1)$$

7-2

have the solution

$$x = \frac{\begin{vmatrix} k_1 & b_1 & c_1 \\ k_2 & b_2 & c_2 \\ k_3 & b_3 & c_3 \end{vmatrix}}{\begin{vmatrix} a_1 & b_1 & c_1 \\ a_2 & b_2 & c_2 \\ a_3 & b_3 & c_3 \end{vmatrix}} \quad \text{etc.;}$$

or more briefly,

$$x = \frac{\begin{vmatrix} k & b & c \end{vmatrix}}{\begin{vmatrix} a & b & c \end{vmatrix}}, \quad y = \frac{\begin{vmatrix} a & k & c \end{vmatrix}}{\begin{vmatrix} a & b & c \end{vmatrix}}, \quad z = \frac{\begin{vmatrix} a & b & k \end{vmatrix}}{\begin{vmatrix} a & b & c \end{vmatrix}},$$

provided $\begin{vmatrix} a & b & c \end{vmatrix} \neq 0$.

To see why this is the case, multiply equations (1) respectively by A_1, A_2, A_3 which are the co-factors of a_1, a_2, a_3 in the determinant $|a\ b\ c|$. Adding the resulting equations, we have

$$(a_1 A_1 - a_2 A_2 + a_3 A_3)x + (b_1 A_1 - b_2 A_2 + b_3 A_3)y$$

$$+ (c_1 A_1 - c_2 A_2 + c_3 A_3)z = k_1 A_1 - k_2 A_2 + k_3 A_3.$$

i.e. $\quad \begin{vmatrix} a & b & c \end{vmatrix}x + \begin{vmatrix} b & b & c \end{vmatrix}y + \begin{vmatrix} c & b & c \end{vmatrix}z = \begin{vmatrix} k & b & c \end{vmatrix}.$

But the second and third terms vanish.

Therefore $\quad \begin{vmatrix} a & b & c \end{vmatrix}x = \begin{vmatrix} k & b & c \end{vmatrix}.$

Since we are assuming that

$$\begin{vmatrix} a & b & c \end{vmatrix} \neq 0,$$

$$x = \frac{\begin{vmatrix} k & b & c \end{vmatrix}}{\begin{vmatrix} a & b & c \end{vmatrix}} \quad \text{as asserted.}$$

The values of y and z are obtained similarly by using the co-factors of their coefficients.

In review, the above brief discussion shows how the solution to a system of simultaneous equations may be written down in determinants and how the determinants may be evaluated.

II. MATRICES

1. Definitions

The notation employed represents

$$a_{11}x_1 + a_{12}x_2 + a_{13}x_3 = k_1,$$
$$a_{21}x_1 + a_{22}x_2 + a_{23}x_3 = k_2,$$
$$a_{31}x_1 + a_{32}x_2 + a_{33}x_3 = k_3,$$

in the form
$$\begin{bmatrix} a_{11} & a_{12} & a_{13} \\ a_{21} & a_{22} & a_{23} \\ a_{31} & a_{32} & a_{33} \end{bmatrix} \begin{bmatrix} x_1 \\ x_2 \\ x_3 \end{bmatrix} = \begin{bmatrix} k_1 \\ k_2 \\ k_3 \end{bmatrix}. \tag{1}$$

The rectangular scheme of coefficients a_{ij} detached from the variables x_j to which they refer, is called the matrix. It may be briefly referred to as A or $[a_{ij}]$. The matrix then is a scheme of detached coefficients. It is a complete entity like a position in chess. For brief reference equation (1) may be summarized as

$$Ax = k.$$

2. Operations

Two matrices A and B of the same order $m \times n$ (i.e. m rows, n columns) may be *added* by adding corresponding elements to form the sum matrix designated $A + B$, i.e.

$$A + B = [a_{ij}] + [b_{ij}] = [a_{ij} + b_{ij}].$$

To multiply a matrix A by a scalar number k, *multiply* all elements a_{ij} by k, i.e.
$$k . A = k[a_{ij}] = [k . a_{ij}].$$

Matrix multiplication[1]

In familar algebra where $z = by$, $y = ax$, we obtain the result $z = bax$ by an operation which we may refer to as multiplication of transformations. When we do this with sets of transformations, we again say that the transformations are multiplied in a certain order

---

[1] Matrix multiplication will be found to be non-commutative, requiring a distinction between pre- and post-multiplication.

and the matrix of the resultant transformation is called the product matrix BA by analogy with ba. It is important to note that multiplication is possible only if *the number of columns in B is the same as the number of rows in A*.

The element in the ith row and jth column of the product matrix BA is obtained by multiplying the elements in the ith row of B into the corresponding elements of the jth column of A, and summing the products so obtained. If B is of order $m \times n$ and A is of order $n \times p$, then $BA = C$, where C is of order $m \times p$, and[1]

$$c_{ij} = \sum_{k=1}^{n} b_{ik} a_{kj}.$$

Unit Matrix

In equation (1), if all elements in the principal (northwest to southeast) diagonal of $[a_{ij}]$ are unity and all other elements zero, we have the unit matrix I. By the rule of matrix multiplication, it will be seen that $IA = AI = A$ although if A is rectangular of order $m \times n$, then the pre-multiplying I must be of order $m \times m$, but the post-multiplying I of order $n \times n$.

A matrix of the form $k.I$ is called a scalar matrix.

$$k.I = \begin{bmatrix} k & . & . \\ . & k & . \\ . & . & k \end{bmatrix}$$

by the rule of scalar multiplication.

3. The adjugate matrix and the inverse

The *adjugate matrix* is the matrix whose elements are the co-factors $|A_{ij}|$ of elements a_{ij} of the square matrix A, but with rows and columns *transposed*, i.e. first row becomes first column, second row second column, etc.

$$\text{Adjugate matrix} = [|A_{ij}|]' = [|A_{ji}|] \equiv \text{Adj } A.$$

Its determinant is called the adjugate determinant of A. Forming the product of the square matrix A and its adjugate, we find:

$$A.(\text{Adj}.A) = |A|.I, \tag{2}$$

[1] See A. C. Aitken, *Determinants and Matrices*, London, 1949.

for as in the following example all non-diagonal elements in the product vanish being expansions in terms of alien co-factors, while diagonal elements are expansions of $|A|$ in terms of row and proper co-factors, e.g.

$$\begin{bmatrix} a_{11} & a_{12} & a_{13} \\ a_{21} & a_{22} & a_{23} \\ a_{31} & a_{32} & a_{33} \end{bmatrix} \begin{bmatrix} |A_{11}| & |A_{21}| & |A_{31}| \\ |A_{12}| & |A_{22}| & |A_{32}| \\ |A_{13}| & |A_{23}| & |A_{33}| \end{bmatrix} = \begin{bmatrix} |A| & . & . \\ . & |A| & . \\ . & . & |A| \end{bmatrix}$$

So long as the determinant $|A|$—comprising the elements of the square matrix A—is not zero, we can divide (2) through by $|A|$ to obtain

$$A . \left\{ \frac{\text{Adj. } A}{|A|} \right\} = I,$$

where by an obvious analogy, the expression in curled brackets is called the inverse of A, or A^{-1}.

4. Solution of simultaneous equations

For the system of n linear equations in n unknowns at the start of this section

$$Ax = k$$

then, assuming the determinant is not zero, by premultiplying both sides by the inverse of A we obtain

$$Ix = x = \left\{ \frac{[|A_{ji}|]}{|A|} \right\} . k.$$

In summary, we can write out the solution to the system of equations in general form, by writing down the inverse. Two examples follow

Example 1. $\qquad 0\cdot1x_1 + \quad x_2 = k_1,$

$$0\cdot2x_1 + 0\cdot1x_2 = k_2.$$

$$A = \begin{bmatrix} 0\cdot1 & 1 \\ 0\cdot2 & 0\cdot1 \end{bmatrix}.$$

$$\text{Adjugate (transposed)} = \begin{bmatrix} 0\cdot1 & -1 \\ -0\cdot2 & 0\cdot1 \end{bmatrix},$$

$$|A| = -0\cdot19.$$

$$\text{Inverse} = \begin{bmatrix} -\dfrac{0\cdot1}{0\cdot19} & \dfrac{1}{0\cdot19} \\[2ex] +\dfrac{0\cdot2}{0\cdot19} & -\dfrac{0\cdot1}{0\cdot19} \end{bmatrix}.$$

So
$$\begin{cases} x_1 = -\dfrac{0\cdot1}{0\cdot19}k_1 + \dfrac{1}{0\cdot19}k_2, \\[2ex] x_2 = \dfrac{0\cdot2}{0\cdot19}k_1 - \dfrac{0\cdot1}{0\cdot19}k_2. \end{cases}$$

Example 2. Obtain the inverse (refer page 15) of

$$\begin{bmatrix} 1 & -50 & 0 & 0 \\ 0 & 1 & 0 & 0 \\ 0 & -20 & 1\cdot5 & -0\cdot5 \\ 0 & -60 & -0\cdot005 & 1 \end{bmatrix}.$$

The adjugate matrix is (transposing as we go)

$$\begin{bmatrix} 1\cdot4975 & 74\cdot875 & 0 & 0 \\ 0 & 1\cdot4975 & 0 & 0 \\ 0 & 50 & 1 & 0\cdot5 \\ 0 & 90\cdot1 & 0\cdot005 & 1\cdot5 \end{bmatrix}.$$

The determinant is $1\cdot4975$ by inspection.

The inverse is

$$\begin{bmatrix} 1 & 50 & 0 & 0 \\ 0 & 1 & 0 & 0 \\ 0 & 33\cdot39 & 0\cdot667 & 0\cdot33 \\ 0 & 60\cdot17 & \cdot003 & 1 \end{bmatrix}.$$

LIST OF SYMBOLS

a_{ni} labour input (n) per unit of commodity (i)

C volume of consumption expenditure at constant prices; C_i quantity of consumption demand of commodity i

D_i final demand for commodity i in physical units: of which $D(h)_i$ is home-produced and $D(m)_i$ is imported supply of the commodity

$D(f)$ non-competing imports satisfying home final demand

E quantity of export demand

F non-competing imports

G government spending on goods and services

H_i total home final demand (quantity)

h_{ii} input co-efficient for home produced internal sales of commodity i to industry i

I investment demand in real terms

M_i imports of commodity i

M_{ii} intermediate demand by industry i for competing imports of commodity i

$\hat{M}_{ij}$ intermediate demand by other industries j for competing imports of commodity i

m_i import coefficient relating imports to home production

N employment

P_i price of commodity i

PDI personal disposable income

P_n wage rate

r interest rate

S profits

s % profit mark-up on wages

t tax rate

W wages

ω work force

X national output; X_i, X_j output of commodities i and j respectively; X_c output of consumer goods, X_e output of investment goods (equipment)

X_{FE} full employment output

x_{ij} input of commodity i used in producing a unit of commodity j

Y national income; Y' national income divided by a price index

BIBLIOGRAPHY

Barna, T. (ed.), *The Structural Interdependence of the Economy* (Varenna, 1954), Wiley & Sons, New York, 1956.

Barna, T. (ed.), *Structural Interdependence and Economic Development,* (Geneva, 1961), Macmillan, London, 1963.

Bruno, M. *Interdependence, Resource Use and Structural Change in Israel,* Bank of Israel, Jerusalem, 1962.

Chenery, H. B. & Clark, P. *Interindustry Economics,* Wiley & Sons, New York, 1962.

Dorfman, R., Samuelson P. A. & Solow, R. *Linear Programming and Economic Analysis,* McGraw-Hill Book Co., New York, 1958.

Heady, E. O. & Candler, W. *Linear Programming Methods,* Ames, Iowa State College Press, 1958.

Koopmans, T. (ed.), *Activity Analysis of Production and Allocation,* Cowles Commission Monograph No. 13, Wiley & Sons, New York, 1951.

Leontief, W. *The Structure of American Economy, 1919–1939,* (2nd ed.), Oxford University Press, 1951.

Leontief, W. (ed.), *Studies in the Structure of the American Economy,* Oxford University Press, 1953.

United Nations, Report of First Group of Experts, *Programming Techniques for Economic Development,* E.C.A.F.E., 60.II.F.3, Bangkok, 1960.

Walras, L. *Elements of Pure Economics,* translation of 1926 edition by W. Jaffé, Allen & Unwin, London, 1954.

INDEX

adjugate matrix, 102
aggregation problem, 30, 33, 36

balance of payments equilibrium, 82

Cobb–Douglas production function, 42
co-factors, 97
competing imports, 28, 31
constant scale returns, 41, 42
consumer tastes, 58
consumption function, 6, 7, 8
costing methods of production, 53
Cramer's rule, 99

demand functions, 10, 58, 64
determinants, 96
development plans, 16, 17, 70
disposable income, personal, 7

efficient activities, 43, 46
employment multiplier, 14
employment, theory of, 4
equilibrium commodity prices, 13, 17
equipment stock, 76, 94

factor content of final demand, 24, 26
factor-supply ratio, 49, 93
factor-use ratio, 49, 93
final product, maximization, 46, 48, 50, 53
foreign trade, 7, 82
full employment output, 6

Gauss–Seidel method of solution, 34
government expenditure, 7

Hecksher–Ohlin case, 89

imports, 28
import substitution, 32
income effect, 66
income multiplier, 12
index function, 63
inverse, 102
investment, 2, 5, 6

isoquant curve, 44, 48
iterative solution, 34

joint products, 39

Keynes, J. M., 4

List, Friedrich, 92

marginal propensity to consume, 7
marginal rate of substitution, 63
matrices, 101
minors, 97
multiplier analysis, 6

national income, 2, 4
non-competing imports, 28, 29, 31
numéraire, 54, 55, 60

'open' input-output model, 14, 16
output, 2, 4, 6, 8, 10, 13

prices, 11, 13, 17, 53, 57, 59, 64, 79, 93, 94
production function, 41
profits, 8, 17

rate of interest, 78, 80
Ricardian case, 84

scalar multiplication, 102
shadow prices of factors, 55, 58, 59, 60, 78, 94
substitution effect, 66
substitution function, 63

tastes, 58, 62
technology, 12, 40, 71, 82, 89
    optimal, 49, 76
transactions table, 2, 19
    compilation, 19
    double-celled, 28
    valuation basis, 22
triangulation of transactions table, 34

utility function, 63